THE IN

Betty Shine is known world<del>wide</del> <del>as a medium</del> and healer. A former opera singer, she has been a medium, healer and hypnotherapist for 25 years, and a vitamin and mineral therapist for over 40 years. She is a regular columnist for the *Daily Mail*, a well-known television and radio personality, and has been invited to lecture all over the world. This groundbreaking new book follows a string of highly successful publications – her compelling autobiography *My Life as a Medium*, her inspirational *A Mind of Your Own* and her delightful and practical *The Little Book of Cosmic Colour*, all published by HarperCollins.

Betty Shine

THE INFINITE MIND

The Mind/Brain Phenomenon

HarperCollins*Publishers*

HarperCollinsPublishers
77–85 Fulham Palace Road
Hammersmith, London W6 8JB
www.**fire**and**water**.com

This paperback edition published 2000
1 3 5 7 9 8 6 4 2

Published by HarperCollinsPublishers 1999

ISBN 0 00 653104 0

Set in PostScript Linotype Bembo by
Rowland Phototypesetting Ltd,
Bury St Edmunds, Suffolk

Printed and bound in Great Britain by
Omnia Books Limited, Glasgow

CONTENTS

I would like to dedicate this book
to my granddaughter
RAINA
for her constant love and support.

'Those who do not give time to the thought attack the thinker.'

PAUL VALÉRY

INTRODUCTION

T WENTY-FIVE YEARS AGO, I discovered an energy around
the head that reacted to every emotion and every thought.
I decided to call it Mind Energy. Further study, through my
abilities as a medium and healer, has given me positive proof that
this energy is not only the powerhouse that drives the brain, but
an indestructible force that survives the death of the physical body
(which includes the brain) and which holds, for ever, the records
of past and present lives.

No one can deny the incredible feats that the brain can achieve
in conjunction with Mind Energy, but eventually, like the rest of
the body, the brain will deteriorate and die. At this point, Mind
Energy leaves and goes back to the source, the Universal Mind.

Brain surgeons, of course, understand the brain and its various
biological functions. I do not. They, in turn, do not understand
the mind. How can they? Unless they have a particular clairvoyant
gift enabling them to see this energy, they cannot study it. But I
have studied Mind Energy for a quarter of a century, and during
that time I have proved the incredible part it plays in the stimulation of the brain and the central nervous system. The scientific
and medical establishments ignore this and continue to tell us that
the memory is in the brain, and constantly use the word 'brain'
when they mean 'mind', and vice versa. The brain is divided up

into different sections which, when triggered by the mind, carry out various functions that stimulate physical reactions. But it is purely physical.

Take the examples of those whose brains, whether through injury or disease, have been permanently affected, yet have been able to communicate and function as though nothing had happened. Although the medical profession has confessed to being puzzled when this happens, I am not surprised, because through my work as a medium and healer I know that everything is recorded first of all in the mind. If the memory *is* stored in the brain, how do I receive messages from the co-called dead? After all, in these people the brain has ceased to be.

No matter how sceptical professionals may be, they can no longer ignore the incredible evidence that mediums have given over hundreds of years. If they do, they are fools. The mind is energy and cannot be destroyed. It is everlasting. It is able to communicate 'mind to mind' with the living, giving proof of survival.

The work of mediums should be recognised as a branch of physics because we study and work with energy structures and the Universe. Unless scientists work closely with intelligent mediums they will never find the Universal answers they are looking for.

At some time in the future, scientists, physicians, mediums and healers will have to work together to perfect the science of whole healing. Many ordinary people throughout the world know the truth, so why then can the scientific community not accept it? Academic training is not enough. There is so much that we do not know, and if we cannot exchange information without prejudice, we will continue in the stalemate position that we have suffered for so long. This would be an immense loss to future generations.

I have friends from every walk of life, and those who have nothing to lose but everything to gain by my teachings are the most adept at changing their lives. They replace negativity with a positive lifestyle, because they overcome their fear of death. They know the mind cannot die, and therefore they enjoy living. They no longer believe that death is the end and lead happier more effective lives because of that knowledge.

I have worked with many doctors and scientists over the years, but they have never been able to tell anyone of their association with me for fear of reprisals from their own profession. Similarly, the lives of many eminent people have been changed because of the help they have received from me, and we have become close friends in the process, but they do not willingly want their names linked with mine. I understand their reticence when it comes to owning up to this particular friendship. Why should they be the butt of ill-mannered jokes? But I believe that it is time for change. It is time to listen and learn from each other – we are all individuals, and as such, should be given the respect we deserve. It is time to co-operate and make the world a better place for everyone, especially innocent children about to enter this very troubled environment.

I have received world-wide recognition for my work on Mind Energy, for which I am truly thankful. I know that I am respected by all who have read my books, or who have met me personally, and that is why I decided to write this book. I want to build bridges, and to teach the world the difference, once and for all, between the mind and the brain.

I would like to thank all those celebrities and sportsmen mentioned by name in this book, for helping me to end the unnecessary stigma suffered by people in my profession. They are all honest, courageous individuals, who long for a more understanding and kinder world for themselves and their families. I would also like to thank those of my friends who have allowed me to use their stories and names in this book. They also deserve their badge of honour, and that is what we should all be seeking – the honour of our respective professions.

I hope this book will make people think twice before they criticise others. I hope it will bring light into the lives of those who are suffering, and those who are terminally ill and fear death. My book is about hope, understanding and love, but most important of all, it is about the survival of the mind, when the physical body and brain have ceased to be.

There is no such thing as death. We have all lived before and we are all going to experience new lives. We simply cannot lose.

1

THE LINK – BOBBY KEETCH

THE EXPERIENCES DESCRIBED in the first chapters of this book are quite remarkable. They concern the lives of famous footballers, past and present, and the way in which I have been used over the past twenty years or so to bring them all together. The experiences are especially amazing, when you consider that I know absolutely nothing about football!

It is well known that footballers look after their own. But through my mediumship and healing I have found that this closeness does not end when they die.

I was enjoying a casual telephone chat with my friend Anne McMenemy one day, when a man with blond hair materialised before me. Interrupting my conversation with Anne, he told me that his name was Bobby, and that he had died from a heart attack and wanted to speak to his wife. He was worried about her. When I repeated this message to Anne, she told me that it was Bobby Keetch, the footballer, who had died recently from a stroke and heart attack. Although Anne was shaken by this, she would probably have been more shocked if she and her husband Lawrie had not been given survival evidence by me when we had first met at a dinner party given by my publisher, Eddie Bell. Anne promised that she would get in touch with Bobby Keetch's wife

Jan, explain what had happened, and leave the decision to her as to whether she wished to contact me or not. I was happy about that because I had no desire to add to my workload unnecessarily.

Half an hour later Jan called me, there was an immediate response from Bobby, and a three-way conversation was soon underway. Bobby was so excited to be speaking to his wife that I mentally had to ask him to slow down, so that I could understand what he was saying. Much later, when the private messages were over, he told us that when he had died he had been met by Bobby Moore and by some of the Manchester United team who had died in the Munich air disaster in 1958. I could hardly believe it. This was the first time that Bobby Moore's name had ever been mentioned, either during survival evidence or speaking to my friends connected with the football world. And what was he doing with the Manchester United team?

Bobby Keetch told me that Bobby Moore and the others were in fact looking after him, and that they had made it possible for him to contact his wife through me. He said that Bobby Moore and his Manchester United friends were going to change the face of football. I was given no clue at this time as to the method they were going to use. It will be interesting to note, for what comes later, that this happened in 1996.

Bobby Keetch also told us that Bobby Moore would like to send a message to his wife, telling her that he had the Afghan hound with him, and to give her his love. Then Bobby Moore actually appeared with his arm around his dog. At this point I had to laugh. When Jan asked me what I was laughing at, I told her that I thought an Afghan hound was the least likely dog to be owned by a footballer. Jan could not shed any light on whether or not Bobby Moore had indeed owned an Afghan hound but, as Stephanie Moore was a friend, she promised that she would ask her about the dog.

At this point Bobby Keetch returned to his conversation with Jan. He said, 'I'm leaving now, but you must never feel alone. I will be with you always.' Then he told her to look at his portrait at the top of the stairs whenever she felt sad. Jan did not understand this. Although there were many pictures of Bobby around the house, there was no portrait in that particular place. But here the messages ended. Jan and I spoke for some time after this, as I felt that I should reassure her that this kind of communication was, for me, an everyday occurrence. We decided to talk again once she had had time to come to terms with what she had been given.

I sat quietly for a while after Jan had rung off. It had been a very emotional, inspiring and informative session, and had come out of the blue, during an ordinary conversation with a friend.

Why had Bobby Keetch been inspired to contact me? The reason is quite simple. Bobby Moore has been in the other dimension for some time, since his death from cancer in 1993, and he had been drawn toward a fellow footballer because minds link with like minds. He would have helped Bobby Keetch by explaining the rather abrupt departure of his mind from his physical body, and how it had entered another dimension. No one could understand that more than the victims of the Munich disaster, so he had been surrounded by the best help that anyone can have when they die. They would have nurtured him and, to help him recover, had taken the opportunity to point him in the right direction when they realised how important it was for him to be able to speak to his wife. Bobby Moore had directed him to me for obvious reasons, and had achieved this by breaking into the conversation I was having with Anne McMenemy.

Since this contact with Bobby Moore I have had many conversations with him, and I have seen him quite clearly when he has manifested to me. He has given me clairvoyance on football matters several times, and on each occasion he has been proved to be correct. I have been able to pass messages on for him, but it is extremely difficult for me to pass on messages to people who do not know me, so some of them have to wait. I do not want to be caught up in sensationalist publicity, and neither do the recipients.

What I can tell you is that the 'team' are extremely concerned about a game that they loved, and obviously still do. Bobby Moore told me that greed is killing off the talent, and the game cannot survive in its present state. He told me that prominent footballers of the future will, because of their fortunes, carry a huge burden. Because of the enormous influence they will have on the next generation, they will have to be seen to be clean, to behave in a manner that will be a credit to their profession. No matter how good a footballer may be, he will be dispatched if his actions do not affect the fans in a positive manner. Bobby told me that the changes will be enormous and will completely alter the concept of football as he knew it, but that, in the end, it would be for the good of all.

He was particularly forthcoming about the future of the charities that would benefit from football. He believed that a new charity should be formed to help footballers who had hit hard times through injuries they received, either as a result of their careers or in general. As he put it, 'When they are fit they give their all. Please don't forget them when they need support.'

Bobby Keetch and Jan have had many conversations through my mediumship, and the love and advice that he has given her and their children has enabled them to deal with their grief in a positive, optimistic way.

I learnt that Bobby Keetch began his career with the London School Boys under 15s before joining West Ham in 1958. From April 1959 to May 1966 he was at Fulham, before moving to Queen's Park Rangers, where he played until 1969. His football career ended with two years playing for Durban City in South Africa.

In 1971 Bobby began his business career which eventually took him into publishing. Bobby and his partner Terry had an idea for a football theme restaurant, and they realised this dream and had a wonderful opening night before Bobby so tragically died.

Jan's story

I received a phone call from my friend Annie McMenemy. She told me that she had been talking to someone called Betty Shine and that a spirit entity had interrupted the conversation by telling her that he had died of a heart attack and wanted to speak to his wife. Betty also said that the man in question had blond hair. Annie told me that she had been shocked, but had immediately recognised that it was my Bobby. She told Betty that he had only passed away a couple of weeks ago. Betty did not know who Bobby Keetch was, and she did not know me either, so this was quite incredible evidence. Annie then told me that Betty would like to speak with me. I called her, and the contact with Bobby was made. It was quite amazing, because neither Betty, nor anyone else, could have known about any of the details of that deeply private conversation.

One thing I did not understand was the instruction to look at the painting at the top of the stairs. What painting? There was nothing at the top of the stairs. But Bobby had been adamant that when I needed him I was to look at this painting.

Months later, a dear friend who knew nothing about this matter presented me with a painting of my husband, and we decided to hang it at the top of the stairs. By this time I had completely forgotten about Bobby's message.

One day, when I was very sad, I was looking at the painting, alternately crying and talking to it. Then it just seemed to come alive. It is quite difficult to explain what happened, but the facial expressions changed, quite literally, and Bobby seemed to be talking to me. And then I remembered his message, '*Look at the painting when you need me.*' And there he was, as he always was, when I needed him. This phenomenon has continued to this day. The facial changes in the picture are quite remarkable, and are definitely not my imagination. But I am the only one who can see these changes taking place. It is just for me.

I have to say that this contact has completely changed my life, and I am content in the thought that Bobby will be there waiting for me when it is my turn to join him, and we will be together again.

Betty Shine has become a very dear friend, and my family and I cannot thank her enough for the gift that she has given us.

Incidentally, Bobby Moore's wife confirmed that they had indeed had an Afghan hound, but that it had originally belonged to her before they were married. It is a mere detail, but it proves beyond any shadow of doubt that the mind of every living thing survives. It was Bobby Moore's way of giving vital, foolproof evidence of survival, because Jan and Bobby Keetch had never known about the dog, and I could certainly never have known about it.

It was also quite remarkable that he had teamed up with the Manchester United team, and quite a shock to me to hear about them again after so many years. They had obviously looked after him when he had left this dimension behind and Bobby Keetch was able to tell us that he had also been cared for by them. He told Jan and I that he had joined this remarkable band of footballers, and was helping them in their work.

Although Jan Keetch and I have since become very close friends, we do not have regular contact because we are both very busy, but whenever there is a problem to be solved her husband appears and asks me to get in touch with her. He has made it clear that he is always there by her side, loving her, protecting her and advising her. This has made a great difference to Jan's life, because she can now live her own life to the full without fear of the future.

I have given the football connection a great deal of thought over the years, as neither myself nor any of my family had ever been remotely interested in the game. Our world was connected to the theatre, to opera and classical music, a far cry from the football fraternity! I have therefore come to the conclusion that it is my complete ignorance of the sport that ensures the quality of the survival evidence. One has to understand that mediums are at their best when they do not know their sitters or those giving survival evidence. This is because there is no possibility of the medium's subconscious blocking the conversation.

I have been fascinated by the mind from the moment I began experimenting with remote viewing more than thirty years ago. The more I learn, the less I seem to know. There is no beginning and no end. The mind is a phenomenon in itself.

The one sure thing that I *have* been able to establish is that the part of the brain which governs memory, like all its other functions, only exists because of its interaction with the mind. Our permanent and indestructible memory storage system is in the mind, proven by the fact that a large part of the brain can be destroyed and yet the personality and memory remain. Even when the brain has died, the mind lives on, communicating and achieving our destiny in another dimension.

2

THE MESSAGE – ALAN HUDSON

WHILST READING THE *Daily Mail* one morning in January 1998, my eye was drawn to a small photograph of a man. The few words underneath told me that the photograph was of Alan Hudson, an ex-footballer. Apparently he had been left severely injured and in a coma after a car had knocked him down having mounted the pavement where he had been walking. Just then, a very strong male voice said to me, 'Please help me.' Then he said, 'I want you to contact my wife and tell her not to give up on me, that I'm still here.' He then went on to give me intimate details of his private life.

I must admit I had to smile as I wondered, 'Where do I go from here?' I had never even heard of Alan Hudson, although he was obviously well known in the football world.

Then my friend Kevin Keegan came to mind. Perhaps he could point me in the right direction? As I have been friends with Kevin's family for some time, especially with his wife Jean, he did not seem too fazed by what I had to say and he promised to help.

For those of you, like me, who know nothing about football, Alan Hudson had a long and distinguished playing career with Chelsea, Stoke City, Arsenal and the Seattle Sounders in the USA. He was capped for England at both Under 23 and Senior level and won many honours in the game, including FA Cup and European Cup Winners Cup medals. Since retiring as a player he has been involved in coaching and journalism.

Later the same day, I was able to have a conversation with David Connolly, a friend of Alan Hudson. He told me he had always been a sceptic where psychic matters were concerned, but that he was conscious that something very extraordinary was taking place, especially once I was able to pass on to him private information that Alan had given me about his family.

David and I talked for some time, and I was able to help him with some problems of his own, which made it easier for him to pass on Alan's messages to his wife, Anne. I was also able to tell him that Alan had told me that Bobby Moore had met him and was helping him. (After Bobby Keetch, what more confirmation does one need to establish that Bobby Moore is still around!)

I was naturally concerned about whether the messages I had received from Alan would be welcome to Anne, as one never really knows how such communications will be received by the family. After all, they did not know me, and although they could check me out through my books, they might want to dismiss the whole thing as a fantasy. Who could blame them? The evidence Anne was going to receive from David was very specific. All that mattered was that she could accept that it was correct.

The following day I received a call from David who told me that although Anne had been shocked, to say the least, she had confirmed everything that Alan had said about his family. She asked David to tell me that she would be contacting me.

From that time on, David rang every day, and I would pass on messages to Anne from Alan. He was extremely positive, and was constantly reassuring us of his eventual recovery. I was also able to tell David that Alan's dead father was in the spirit dimension, helping him.

Anne's story

My introduction to Betty Shine came within a week of Alan's accident, whilst I was sitting by his bedside in the Intensive Care Unit. Our friend David phoned me and said that he had something to tell me. He seemed a little unsure as to whether he should pass on this information, as the messages were from a medium, but I encouraged him to tell me the whole story.

Apparently Betty Shine had been contacted by Alan after she had seen a photograph of him in the *Daily Mail*. He had asked her to contact me with the message that he was going to recover, despite his terrible injuries. In fact, he was giving us his own diagnosis. This seemed incredible, as his injuries were so bad that the medical team looking after him had said that he was unlikely to pull through, and he was in a coma. Although I had always been very sceptical about such matters, I listened to everything David had to say, as Betty appeared to be extremely accurate, even when detailing the very delicate issues of his injuries.

For four months I was able to give Anne information about her husband's injuries and about how they were progressing. I had to explain, because this information *was* so detailed, that I had a superb team of spirit doctors who were helping me. After all, this was all very new to her. At one point, I was able to alleviate Anne's worst fears by telling her that the swelling in Alan's brain had reduced, which was later confirmed by the medical team.

There were other strange things happening in Alan's family at this time. When his sister Julie was told about his accident she became desperately upset, screaming for her father. As she did so, a gold cross appeared on the wall behind her. It stayed for two days, and was seen by five other people. I believe that when she screamed for her dead father, who was helping Alan, he activated this symbol to give his daughter peace of mind. Julie told Anne that the cross had no shadow – this is quite normal with such phenomena. Spirits do not have shadows either, they *are* the shadows!

Some time later, Julie re-decorated the room, but the incredible energy impact needed to form the cross in the first place had left an indelible mark. The cross remains on the wall.

The role that David took on as the middle-man, passing messages from Alan and myself to Anne, was truly the act of a loyal and loving friend. He kept a diary, and it was only when reading his transcript that I realised just how awful those dark months of December and January had been for Alan's wife, family and friends. Eventually, however, Alan came out of his coma and began the long journey of recovery.

Whilst speaking to David on the phone one day, Alan's paternal grandfather appeared to me and told me that he was helping Alan. I could see him so clearly that I was able to give David a detailed description of him. When this was passed on to Alan he was surprised, because he had never really had much contact with his paternal grandfather. So you see, when people are in trouble, everyone will gather round to help.

David and Anne have since visited me at my home, and we have all become close friends. I have spoken to Alan over the phone and am very excited about his recovery, although he obviously still has a lot of work to do to get back to a hundred per cent. But the fact that he started working again from his hospital bed gives one an insight into the power and personality which enabled him to contact me in the first place.

While he was still in hospital, I told Anne, via David, that one of the medical staff would, when Alan recovered, turn around and say, 'This is nothing short of a miracle.' As time passed, doctors and nurses alike would make remarks about his 'incredible recovery', but Anne told me that she wanted to hear the exact words that I had given her. One day, as the sister was about to leave the room after speaking with Anne for some time, she reached the door, hesitated, then turned around and said, 'This is nothing short of a miracle.' These words convinced Anne that a 'miracle' had taken place, because every word I had passed on to her, even about family matters which at that time had not yet taken place, had come true. The following passage is a continuation of Anne's story:

> There were many times over the next few months when Alan's condition was 'touch and go', but Betty was always there, giving me an exact diagnosis and the outcome, which was always positive. Each time, she was proved right. I began to get a great deal of comfort from her calls throughout the ordeal of the ICU.
>
> It is now May 1998, six months after the accident. Alan is still in hospital but is making good progress, and is on his way to making a full recovery. Both Alan and Betty have been proved right. They were the only people who, right from the start, were positive about the eventual outcome, when everyone around us thought that all was lost. Betty Shine is a very special lady who has helped me immensely. Alan and I cannot thank her enough.

When Alan came out of the coma, he said that he had actually seen his father. He also told me, when I had my first telephone conversation with him, that he had always believed in psychic matters, and that he thought he had certain gifts in this direction. He said something wonderful had happened to him and that he had seen the most beautiful places, and he knew instinctively that these were not hallucinations, that they were real. In a letter he sent to me he wrote that, when he was travelling at high speed in the energy dimension, he passed both his father and a very dear friend who had died.

Those of you who have never had a psychic experience may find it very difficult to come to terms with the fact that the mind is infinite, that it survives death, and that it can take over when the brain has been damaged. But if we did not have a mind that is totally separate from the brain, none of us would exist, because it is the mind that creates the link between the Universal Mind and the brain. We are all children of the Universe; we came from the source, and to the source we will return. There will be more about this later in the book. For the moment, let me assure you that nothing is what it seems, and that anything is possible.

Because of the swelling in Alan's brain, he was reduced to a comatose state. This happens when the messages from brain to body are disrupted, and the mind seeks alternative routes of communication.

Alan's story is typical of the stress that the personality endures when it feels that it can no longer communicate through the brain. The patient does not suffer, because they are in a peaceful and loving environment. Their wish to communicate is driven by the desire to ease the suffering of their friends and family and, in Alan's case, to pass on to them the knowledge that he was going to survive.

As I mentioned earlier, others in the spirit dimension can come forward to ease tension and give proof of survival during these trying times. I was speaking to Anne one day when a man's voice repeated the name Harry several times. I asked her if she knew who this might be, and she told me that her late uncle's name was Harry. I then passed on to her messages of a private nature, which were confirmed. Anne was having a lot of 'firsts' at this time! Having had no previous experience of survival evidence, she told me that she found it a great comfort to have someone of her own communicating with her, especially as she had been Harry's only niece and had been much loved by him. I explained that he had come through so that she would not feel so alone.

The family has asked me to thank all the medical staff at the London Hospital and at St Bartholomew's hospital for all the loving care that Alan received from them during his long stay with them. As a medium, it was a great honour for me to bring the two worlds together, easing the grief of the family as they waited for their loved one to recover from such a terrible trauma.

For me, this is just one of many hundreds of similar stories that are being played out every day, each one as remarkable as the last. I therefore hope that Alan's story will bring hope and comfort to the families of all those who are currently in a coma.

3

MANCHESTER UNITED AND BOBBY MOORE

I WAS FIRST INTRODUCED TO Bobby Moore through my contact with Bobby Keetch, and then again through Alan Hudson. There was an interval of twenty months between these messages. But the first contact I had from the Manchester United team was over twenty years ago.

Out of respect for one particular family, when I wrote about the story of the team's survival in my first book I did not give the actual name of the club. I can reveal it now because of the remarkable circumstances surrounding the footballers mentioned in these chapters, which span so many years. They have made it quite clear that they will not be silenced. They *want* people to know they have survived, and to be happy for them, to replace bad memories with good.

This is the story from *Mind to Mind* which will give some insight as to how I became involved with the Manchester United team some twenty-two years ago.

David was a young amateur footballer who had been turned away from our local hospital because he had broken so many small bones in his feet that they had told him there was nothing more they could do. Crippled and in despair he asked me for an emergency session.

I had met David for the first time when he came to me with a twisted ankle and badly sprained ligaments in his foot. A physiotherapist had treated it with ice-packs, manipulation and ultrasound, and after two weeks he was pronounced fit enough to play again. A month later he sprained it again, this time tearing some tissue around the Achilles tendon. On the advice of friends he visited yet another physiotherapist who used the same methods as the previous one. He was then told that he was fit enough to play. This performance was repeated regularly for the next four years! In all he saw a total of nine different physiotherapists, for various injuries, but the effects were only temporary, until he came to me for healing.

On one particular occasion he had had a very bad kick in the groin. A particularly eminent physiotherapist correctly diagnosed a slight hernia, and fitted him with a makeshift truss. David was told that he would not be able to play for a month or more. He then had a successful healing session with me which cured the hernia, and was playing again the following Saturday.

David's faith in my healing powers were such that when he was told to go home and live with his crippled feet he once again turned to healing. But this time was going to be very different to his previous appointments.

He arrived with his father, who was also a witness to the events that were about to take place. I told David to lie on the couch and I positioned my chair at the end so that I could place my hands on his feet and legs. I had only just begun to heal him when a voice told me to take my hands away. I was not at all fazed by this because it happened quite often during healing sessions with other patients. I took my hands away and moved back from the couch. Then we all three watched in amazement as the injured leg was lifted up, pushed about and thoroughly manipulated. Healing can sometimes be extremely painful, while the body is being energised, and this occasion was no different. David was in considerable pain.

But then something unbelievable happened during the healing, something that only I could hear. A man's voice told me that he had been one of the Manchester United team who had died in the Munich air crash. He told me that he wanted to heal footballers and athletes through me. He had obviously been a very compassionate man when he was alive and wanted to continue to help people in his profession. I consequently tried to contact his family, but was told that their religion did not accept mediumship. I thought this was very sad, as he so obviously wanted to prove his survival. He gave me the names of all those who had died and those who had survived. The evidence, when checked out later, was found to be one hundred per cent correct.

After the manipulation by our footballer friend, David hopped off the couch, completely cured! And from that time on, athletes of every profession who visited me received remarkable cures.

This all happened over two decades ago. And now, here the team were again, first in 1996 and again in 1998.

Bobby Moore let me know that he was the spokesman for the footballers who now found themselves in a quite different environment, but who were happy that, from their viewpoint, they could help the world of football.

He told me that materialism with a non-spiritual format was endangering the game, and endangering the minds and lives of the footballers themselves. He was concerned that the inevitable problems that walk side by side with huge salaries were destroying not only the footballers, but also their wives and families, and that spirituality had to become part and parcel of the game for the sake of everyone involved.

I found this particular viewpoint inspiring, because I had for many years asked the professional sportsmen and women who had regularly visited me for healing to think about this aspect of their life. Those who took my advice and worked on the spiritual side of their lives were extremely successful, both in their careers and in their private lives. I also believe they were motivated by their healing experiences, as many would never have returned to their respective sports careers had it not been for the intervention of healing.

No matter how sceptical the media may be on the subject of healing, it is preferable to the alcohol and drugs that are consumed daily by a large proportion of people who have to spend their lives in the spotlight. Eventually it takes its toll and the brain and physical capabilities are weakened.

It is a common sight to see footballers making the sign of the cross as they enter the stadium and when they leave. They obviously believe in their God and are not ashamed of showing the world that they have asked for help from a spiritual source.

I find it quite incredible that, in this day and age, with the millennium at hand, there are so many closed minds in the world of sport. I have a following of a million or more people around the world, including close friends who are at the top of every profession, who have admitted that their spirituality is the one thing that has enabled them to reach their potential. For it is from the spiritual realms that they receive their inspiration.

I must confess that it always makes me smile when I think of the members of the Manchester team making contact with me, someone they probably would never have consulted in their lifetime, who still cannot remember the names of famous footballers, has never seen a live match, and has no understanding of the rules. In fact, football is as much a mystery to me as my job is to the footballers themselves!

But the one thing that shows itself time and again in these stories is the love of footballers for their families and for their game. Seemingly, neither can die.

I now know the changes that are going to take place within the football world, and it will be interesting to see how the most powerful force of all will create these changes.

I also know that as the players change, so will their followers. There will be a marked difference as the players of the future impress them with their abilities, without the influence of alcohol and drugs. For the power of the mind is the greatest power of all.

4

MEMORIES ARE MADE OF THIS

ALL THE WOMEN FEATURED in this chapter are my friends. They have agreed to describe their impressions of the survival evidence they have received through me and through others because we share a mutual trust; they know how much it means to me to prove the existence of the 'infinite mind'.

I thank them for this and for their courage; they already have had more publicity than most people would like in a lifetime.

I find it strange that so many millions of people worldwide who believe in life after death are still continually subjected to views which are based on blind ignorance. I hope these stories will at least help the blind to see that human beings are extremely adept at sorting the wheat from the chaff and at reaching a logical conclusion.

Nicolette's story

I was thrilled when Nicolette Keetch – Jan's daughter – sent me this account of her telepathic conversations with her father.

No one could have prepared me for the intense pain and feeling of loss when my father died suddenly of a stroke. Amongst many other reasons, it was because I had lost the only person in the world who I felt I could really talk to, and whose advice I completely trusted and respected. The day before my father's death I had experienced the strangest of feelings, severe panic attacks and a premonition that something terrible was going to happen.

I had spoken to my father that morning, and he had asked me to join him for lunch as he was going to have a barbecue. I told him that I had to keep an appointment, but that I would join him as soon as it was over. In the middle of the appointment my mother called to tell me that my father had suffered a stroke. She was, understandably, desperately upset at this point. The strange thing was that the call came through to me on my mobile phone which had not been charged, and to this day I don't know how it picked up the call. I rushed home to be with them both. It was the last time I was ever to see my father alive. He died that evening.

A few months after my father's death, and after receiving survival evidence, Betty, and my mother and I, were guests at a dinner party given by Terry and Toots Venables. Terry and my father had been great friends, and so he and Toots were of course interested in everything that had been happening since he died. Terry himself was to receive survival evidence that evening, which made it a special occasion for all of us. The evening was full of laughter and fun, as my father would have wished. At the end of the evening, my mother offered Betty – who was in London to celebrate the publication of her latest book – a lift back to her hotel.

As soon as we had settled in the car, Betty turned round and told me that my father was sitting beside me and wanted to speak with me. When she relayed his messages, I knew it *was* my father. He spoke about me, my life and aspirations, and I knew there was no way Betty could possibly have known anything about me because we had only met that night. He spoke to me throughout the whole journey, assuring me that he would always be there for me, whenever I needed him. That was two years ago.

Since then, I have felt his strong presence around me on a number of occasions. But the most recent experience was very special. I had finished work, and was on my way to Cardiff where I was meeting my boyfriend, as we were to be guests at my friend's wedding the following day. I was focusing my mind on the journey when, suddenly, I felt my father beside me. The feeling was so strong – as though he had, with great force, projected himself into the passenger seat. At the time it seemed perfectly normal for him to be there, and I began to have a conversation with him. When it was over, I felt that it had lasted for such a short time that I wished it could have continued, but was shocked to find that we had been conversing for two hours. During that time we had laughed and joked as we had before he'd died. It seemed strange, as I could not hear him physically, but inside my mind – telepathically. He also gave me a mental picture of himself, as he used to be, and as I remembered him. It was a lovely night, the sky was very red, and I felt so calm. I felt better than I had done for a very long time.

In the past, when I had been alone, I had often prayed that my father would speak to me, but nothing had happened. Perhaps I had been trying too hard. Now, when he did appear, I had done nothing at all.

Although I had been driving for two hours, I could hardly remember the journey. When I reached Cardiff I felt his presence leave. I arrived at the hotel and was greeted by my boyfriend. We had a drink but I did not mention the experience. It was too new, and I find it easier not to talk about moments that are very precious to me. I want to hug them to me and feel the love that the messages were wrapped in.

I now feel a great sense of relief in knowing that I have not lost that important help and advice that I have missed so much. I know I do not even have to ask for help, that my father will be there for me, as promised, whenever I need him.

I was thrilled by this account because for many years I have been encouraging my clients and readers to accept that we can all have a telepathic link with our loved ones. Although they are existing in a different energy structure to the one we have here, we can, nevertheless, keep our hearts and minds open to the fact that it is possible. If a link is made by loved ones, it should not be dismissed as pure fantasy or wishful thinking. Such a link can be quite dramatic, like Nicolette's, if the recipient is in any way psychic. But it can also be disappointing if any shadow of doubt enters the mind, because doubt can close the mind.

Jean's story

The following two accounts have been contributed by Jean Keegan and her mother, Molly.

My dear friend Anne McMenemy had spoken to me on several occasions about the fascinating evening she had spent with Betty Shine. She had also told me about Betty's incredible healing gifts. I reminded Anne of these conversations when she was suffering severe pain during an illness and told her to ring Betty for help. She was reluctant to do so because she knew that Betty was already inundated with work, so I asked for Betty's telephone number and decided to ring her myself. My thoughts were for Anne. My friend was in trouble, and she needed someone to help her.

When Betty answered the phone, I heard this warm and cheerful voice and felt so relaxed that I just chatted away. I felt as if I had known her all my life. It was incredible how this one action completely changed my life.

It was towards the end of our conversation that Betty suddenly stated that someone was coming through and wanted to speak to me. I went cold from head to foot and began trembling as she described my recently departed father. She gave me evidence that no one on this earth could have known, except Mum, Dad and myself. So many mixed feelings rushed through my body, I didn't know whether to laugh or cry. I missed Dad so much, and here was this wonderful lady – to whom I had spoken for the first time only ten minutes ago – passing on private messages to me and my family, proving that he had survived the trauma of the physical death and was now living 'somewhere else'.

I have always had an open mind about life after death, wanting to believe that we do survive, and that we will eventually meet up with our loved ones again. But without proof it is difficult to believe. I cannot begin to explain how comforting this was. Dad always used to say, when someone passed away, that 'life goes on'. How true those words were proving to be! Now we could all go on, knowing that he was looking after us, as he had done when he was alive.

Towards the end of the messages, Betty asked me if I had any questions for Dad. My mind went a complete blank. All I really wanted to know was if he was happy. There was a short pause, and then Betty said that he was laughing and smiling and holding hands with an older lady, who was looking up at him lovingly. I believe that was my grandmother. As a young boy Dad took care of his mother as she used to have epileptic fits and I know how happy he must feel knowing that she was also at peace. He was home with his long lost family.

I realised then that I had to stop wishing he was back with us. He was, and always will be, a very important part of our lives. He was a wonderful father, and never a day goes by that I do not think of him. Now, through Betty's gifts, I know that I can speak to him. At every family event, special occasions like birthdays and anniversaries, we can feel his presence.

Some weeks later, Betty rang me and told me that Dad was worried about a horse. At this time she did not know we kept horses. She gave me the message, and Dad was, once again, spot on. Her accurate diagnosis and healing of several of our horses showed yet another facet of her talents.

We are now very good friends and often enjoy a good chat.

Molly's story

Whilst Betty and I were talking one day, my husband came through and gave me a whole host of messages. Because of my grief at his death I really did not take it all in, but she gave me one particular message that I have never forgotten, because the minute details she described about a certain situation only my husband and I could have known about. He ended the message with such caring words of wisdom that I was reduced to tears. I have endeavoured to live up to them.

Since then I have read every one of Betty's books, and never go to sleep without reading from them. They have given me such comfort, there is no way I can repay her.

The only sadness in my life is the fact that the power of healing and the comfort of mediumship was unknown to me during my husband's lifetime. It would have helped ease his suffering and pain. At least now he is at peace.

Jean's family and her mother have more than repaid me with their constant and loving friendship.

Toots's story

The final story for this section is from the wife of another footballing personality, Toots Venables.

After the death of my grandmother I decided to go with a friend to visit a Spiritualist church. Neither of us had any kind of previous experience so we did not know what to expect.

We chose seats at the back, and listened as some of the congregation received messages from their loved ones. I was amazed because the recipients seemed to accept the evidence as though it was an everyday occurrence – so laid back and relaxed. Then the medium pointed to me and said, 'I have your grandmother here.'

I must confess I was so shocked that I thought I would faint. I became very emotional, and my eyes filled with tears. The medium told me about things that I could relate to myself and family, but I felt that they could equally have applied to others. Then he told me that my grandmother was saying, 'Ask her about the tomatoes.' When I told him that I had no idea what she was talking about, the medium continued, 'She is saying that she used to do something to her tomatoes that made people laugh.' This was becoming embarrassing because I had to tell him again that I hadn't a clue what she was talking about. He replied, 'Your grandmother is telling me that your mum will know. Ask her.'

After the service, I rushed home to give the message to Mum. When I had finished, she looked at me in amazement, and said, 'Nan used to sprinkle sugar all over her tomatoes – and people did laugh when they saw she did this.'

I knew immediately that the spur of the moment decision to visit the Spiritualist church had changed my whole conception of spirituality, and encouraged me to have a more open mind.

I have also received many messages from my father since he passed away two and a half years ago. These messages are always comforting. The most recent message was given to me by a medium in church. He told me that my dad had worked for London Transport as a bus driver, we came from East Ham, and that he had had an accident in his bus but never told anyone about it. He also told me that my grandad Tom was there, and that he used to work in the docks when they were full of big ships, a real working dock. The medium was absolutely accurate in every detail but one, or so I thought. Yes, we did live in East Ham, and my dad had worked for London Transport for twenty-five years, but neither my mother nor I knew anything about an accident. However, my brother Paul later told me that when he was fourteen he had found Dad's driving licence and had noticed that there was an endorsement on it for an accident that had occurred. My brother had never mentioned this to anyone.

Another message I had from Dad was very funny. We had a wonderful dog called Oscar, and my father really loved him. Every day whilst preparing Oscar's food he would add grated carrot to the meal. During a visit to a medium, she told me, 'I'm getting a message which makes no sense to me at all, but I must give it to you. Your father is telling you not to forget the carrots.' What more proof does one need?

However, my husband Terry was very sceptical about mediums – even though his great-grandmother was a medium herself. His mother Eileen would often tell me stories about her.

When our best friend Bobby Keetch died suddenly, it was not only a great shock to us but to everyone who knew him. He was always so full of life, and was one of the nicest and funniest people we have ever known. On the day after his funeral, Terry and I were going on holiday, but before we left I arranged for Jan and Nicky (Bobby's wife and daughter) to have a sitting with a medium. It was arranged for twelve noon on the following Tuesday.

During our holiday in Bali, I told Terry that I would ring Jan to find out how she had got on. I worked out when to call as there is a six-hour time difference. We had our usual siesta and I woke, feeling slightly disorientated, at about 6.00 p.m. I was amazed to find that not only did we not have a light in the room but the main supply was not working either – and yet on looking out of the window I could see that all the other villas had light. We rang reception, and they were as puzzled about the power cut as we were. Terry then asked me for the time. It was seven o'clock, and with the time difference was exactly when Jan and Nicky were due to visit the medium. I turned to Terry and said, 'I bet that's a sign from Bobby.' Of course, Terry laughed.

Later that evening I rang Jan to find out how she had got on. Her sister-in-law answered the phone and explained that Jan still hadn't returned. I told her about the lights. When Jan got home she told her sister-in-law that the medium had told her Bobby was saying, 'I did the lights, it was me.' But Jan hadn't known what the medium was talking about. We were all amazed by this evidence. And when Bobby contacted Betty whilst she was having a telephone conversation with Anne McMenemy, we knew that he would always be with us.

Many years after the death of Terry's mum, we arranged to have dinner with Betty, Jan and her daughter Nicolette. But whilst we were waiting to be seated at the table, Betty began to give Terry survival evidence that took him back to his childhood. Then she said, 'This lady is cooking something for you. I don't know what it is, but I'm being given a picture of something that is neither a cake or a pancake, it's a "thing" and it's about this big.' Betty then made a size with her hands about four inches in diameter. We were amazed because it was something his mum would always cook with Terry's bacon and eggs for breakfast. It was just flour and water mixed together and fried. There was no name for it, and it was always referred to as 'one of those *things*'. The evidence went on for some time, and was so accurate that Terry changed his opinion about mediums.

One day, whilst I was talking to Betty over the phone, she told me that my dad wanted to speak with me. He gave me wonderful evidence of his survival, and even described the flooding that had taken place that very morning whilst I was using the washing machine.

I do not find mediumship weird or spooky, but comforting. I find the fact that our loved ones are still around and able to communicate with us a bonus, and one that I would miss if it were not available.

The important thing in this life is to have an open mind.

It is important to remember that even though you may not yet have had any evidence of survival, someone is always with you. Love is the greatest link that we have with those who have temporarily left us.

5

MIND TRAVELLING

TINKERING WITH THE MIND REALLY began for me thirty years ago when I lived in Spain. Looking out over the vineyards toward the sea from my vantage point high in the hills, I had time to think for what seemed like the first time in my life. Although the move from England had created many problems, I was able to forget them as I luxuriated in this freedom of thought. It was as though I had found the key that had been lost to me since childhood when, in my innocence, I had been able to open the doors of my mind with ease. However, bringing up a family and pursuing a singing career meant that the key had been mislaid, covered in etheric dust, neglected. Now that I had found it again I was determined to clear away the cobwebs, to polish it and make it work for me.

The sun, shining on the sea in the distance, also opened my heart chakra, allowing suppressed emotions to evaporate with floods of tears. The pain I had endured for seventeen years from a ruptured disc in my spine disappeared, never to be felt again. This alone gave me food for thought. Why had the pain disappeared? I still had the ruptured disc. Nothing had changed but my frame of mind.

Having practised yoga for many years, I had learnt the art of relaxation – or so I thought – so why hadn't that released me from my straitjacket of pain? It was a mystery that I could not solve at that point, but it made me think and encouraged me to open not just one door but several, each taking me down avenues that were exciting, exhilarating – and sometimes frightening.

I remember the day I put myself into daydreaming mode and took the first 'mind walk' from my home to the nearest village. For the first time I saw things that I had never noticed during my physical walks. For instance, the ruts and potholes looked far more menacing than they did when I rode over them on my scooter. The wild herbs were more abundant, and there were tiny wild flowers shining like seed pearls that I had never seen before. They were hidden from the naked eye, and quite beautiful. I was exhilarated by this experience and used my mind to seek and find other things that had been hidden from normal sight.

Turning left, off the path and on to the main road that led to the village and the sea, the view looked strangely unfamiliar. I thought I knew this route like the back of my hand, yet I could see pylons, masts and other strange objects that looked completely out of place. I made a mental note of them to check out later.

When I finally reached the village, I saw three of my friends sitting at a table outside a café, drinking coffee. This was great! It meant that I could check with them later to make sure that my journey was real and not simply a fantasy.

I took off my shoes when I reached the beach, allowing the sand to trickle through my toes, and as I got to the sea I could feel the cold water lapping around my ankles – and this jolted me back into my body again. As I looked around, I could not believe that I was still sitting on the terrace looking out to sea instead of walking barefoot on the beach. It had been an incredible experience, and one that I could not wait to put into practice again.

The next day my friends confirmed my sighting, and asked why I hadn't joined them. Not wishing to go into any detail, I told them I had been in a hurry to return home.

The next time I went into the village, I walked the scooter

down the rutted path and carefully checked the tall grasses where I had seen the tiny flowers. At first I saw nothing, but then I saw them, hidden in the undergrowth like miniature glow-worms. They were exquisite. My excitement mounted as I investigated the abundance of wild herbs. How could I have missed them on my previous journeys? I could have understood it if I had always used motor transport, but I often walked the path and still had not seen them. I vowed to walk more often in the future and pay greater attention, so that I would not miss out on any other jewels of nature.

When I reached the main road I took to my scooter and made my way toward the village. I was very disappointed when I realised that I could not see many of the ugly pylons and masts that I'd noticed on my mind journey. How could this be? Feeling a little despondent, I turned down a side road so that I could survey the scene from a higher vantage point. And there they were! From the road they had been completely hidden behind the pine trees. I became very excited as I realised that my mind travelling had been on a higher level than my physical travelling and that something could leave my body and hover above the earth, leaving an impression on my mind. Unlike a dream, I remembered *every* detail.

My quest had begun. Every day I put aside some time for my mental travels, following them up with the physical journey and checking all the way. I sometimes found myself taking small paths that I would never have dreamt of exploring alone, experiencing for the first time a freedom and a sense that I belonged with the birds, gliding along on the shifting currents of air.

Every time I took a mind journey something else happened, too. I felt a tingling sensation sweeping through the whole of my body, which energised me for several days.

Those years spent practising the art of mind travelling were some of the most fascinating and happy times I have ever known. Strangely, I never thought that I was linking into something new, but felt only sadness that I had neglected the art for so long. Somewhere inside, I knew that I had done it all before.

Whether my experiments with mind travel had reached out into the Universe and touched other minds I do not know, but I was certainly not prepared for what happened next.

One beautiful moonlit night, my first husband Leslie was standing on the terrace of our villa when he called to my daughter Janet and me to join him. He sounded very excited as we hurried out, only for him to point out a small bright star in the night sky. Disappointed, I remarked that it was just a star. 'Look closer,' he said. 'It's moving around in circles.'

We stood quietly for a few minutes, observing the bright light, and it soon became clear that something unusual *was* happening. Not only was the star moving in ever increasing circles, but it was also increasing in size. Then suddenly it was upon us, hovering over the villa. I saw blue porthole windows, shining with an eerie light, but what frightened me most was its size. It was huge. I felt menaced by this shining object – but then anything unusual dropping out of the sky would give one the same feeling! Anyway, I was not going to hang around, and neither was Janet. We both rushed indoors and locked the doors, leaving my poor husband outside to meet his fate! Then the humming sound stopped, and I gathered enough courage to open the door and look out. The strange object had gone. I asked Leslie what had happened, and he told me that it had disappeared as soon as I had gone indoors.

When we discussed the experience later, it became clear to the three of us that we all had different perceptions of what we had seen. My description perhaps was far more detailed and of something much bigger than that of the others. Perhaps my mind went out to meet it, I will never know. For me the vision has never dimmed, for I have seen three UFOs since that first visit.

★　★　★

My life was never the same after that. I experienced recurring choking sensations and my body seemed to have gone completely out of sync. My mother, who had been dead for several years, materialised in my bedroom, as did other entities who seemed to appear out of nowhere. I realise now, of course, that the power from the UFO had opened up my psyche, but at the time it was very unsettling.

Following the UFO experience I also found that I could leave my body just by thinking about it. It was fantastic. Everyday I explored a different part of the coastline. I found that from a great height I could descend rapidly, like a bird, which meant that I could survey the houses and farmhouses in remote areas. I did not know at the time that this kind of phenomenon was called an Out-of-Body Experience. It is quite a different sensation to that of projecting the mind along a specific path. With OBEs, as they are called, there is a realisation that we have the ability to fly, not physically, but with the mind. Although at this stage in my life I had not even begun to think of the mind, as such, I just knew that there was something that could indeed leave the physical body and 'fly'. I accepted this as if it were the most natural thing in life, perhaps because I had been so adept in my childhood.

At this time in Spain, many of my friends left their villas unattended when they made their frequent return visits to England. As I was a permanent resident, they asked me to look after their properties for them, and I was happy to do this – until eventually the requests mounted so that it was impossible to keep an eye on them all at once. So I resorted to mind projection. By using this technique I was able to visit the villas every day, and made a rota for my less frequent physical visits. There were times when I wondered whether I was putting too much faith in this gift – until one day, whilst mentally visiting one of the villas, I saw two men looking at the outside and another trying to force the front door. I immediately raced down the rough path from my villa on my scooter and notified a friend, who called the

Guardia Civil. They apprehended two of the men, and after that I never doubted my mind pictures.

For the first time in my life, I had lots of time at my disposal so I looked at the building work that was being carried out in the surrounding hills. I was shocked not only by the way the villas were being built, but how the hills were being raped. Where there had once been beautiful foliage and wild flowers, there were now great gaping holes of red earth, piles of rubble, concrete blocks with which the villas were built, and old tractors and vehicles that could scarcely make their way up the hills. Using mind projection, I used to home in on the work that was being carried out, and was amazed to see workmen shoving tin cans into the gaps where they had misjudged the space between the concrete, and then pointing over it to make it look normal. Beer cans galore went into those buildings, plus any other rubbish that had been left behind, but when the workmen had finished, the villas looked beautiful. I wondered how many years the beer cans would last before everything collapsed. When I was building my own villa I made sure that I visited the site every day, and I don't think any beer cans went into its construction. But who knows?

This detective work led to my looking at the structure of buildings in general, and when I became a medium I was able to use this gift to help those who were thinking of buying a property. I remember having a drink with a friend who was also my bank manager. He asked me to survey a house he was going to buy. I believe he was testing me, as he had already had it surveyed in the proper manner. When I told him how many slates were missing on the roof, and of a possible problem with the damp-proof course on the corner of the house, he was amazed. His survey had not mentioned these things. But on checking he found that what I had said was correct. I was also able to take him from room to room and described the house internally. I don't think he ever got over the shock. I admit that I do have an added advantage in being able to survey the properties from an aerial view!

After the visit from the UFO it seemed that everything in my life had changed, and not for the better. Now, of course, I can see that it was part of a larger plan that I could not possibly have envisaged at that moment. If someone then had given me a clairvoyant vision of my future, I would have thought that they were stark staring mad.

The time came, however, when I had to sell my villa and return to England. I had no idea what I would do, or where I was going to live. My singing career was over, and although I have many interests I did not want to follow them up professionally. I also have a low boredom threshold, so I knew that I would have to find something pretty exciting to do. I had no idea that someone in the spiritual dimension had already earmarked a career for me, a career that would keep me on my toes until the day I die. Neither did I realise that the word 'boredom' would never be part of my vocabulary again.

There were several things I was going to miss: the time for mind travelling, the weather, the peace and isolation, the glorious views – and last but certainly not least my beloved pets. The kindest thing I could do was to have them put to sleep. They were so loved that they would never have survived quarantine, and the cruelty toward all animals in Spain made it impossible for me to hand them on to others. (This story is told in *Mind to Mind*.)

I also worried about the beautiful stray dogs that roamed the area. Every night I put out several large trays of rice for them, mixed with other bits and pieces of nourishing food. I tried to make their life happy while it lasted. They were all eventually shot. This was understandable in some ways, as rabies was a very real fear in Europe in those days. But with modern methods of treating wild animals the future looks brighter and, hopefully, rabies will soon be a thing of the past.

But my memories of Spain always retain that imprint of cruelty towards animals. I know that I could never live there again, unless the laws concerning animals were changed. There was a lot of pain in my heart when I left Spain for good.

Little did I know that I had inadvertently taken a path from which there would be no return. It is obvious to me in retrospect that, having once opened the mind and spent time perfecting the art of mind travelling and OBEs, there could be no turning back. Fortunately, because my paternal grandmother had been a medium and the talent was obviously passed on, I have been able to spend the last twenty-five years perfecting the art. It has been a privilege that I have never abused.

6

HOME AGAIN

WHEN I RETURNED TO ENGLAND I found it hard to settle down at first, and the weather did not help one bit! I had forgotten the grey skies that hung suffocatingly overhead.

I was also unnerved by the fact that the flat we rented for a short time was haunted.

For those of you who have not read the accounts in my previous books, I will give a few details of the strange things that happened in this apartment: heavy, old-fashioned wardrobe doors were thrown across the room like matchwood; taps would be mysteriously turned off; blue lights appeared and danced around the bedroom; whispering voices could be heard at night; and articles of clothing disappeared all the time.

I had never been involved in paranormal activities. In fact, other than my own experiences I had never given the occult world a single thought – my life had always seemed light years away from such things. Or so I thought. When we realised that these 'happenings' weren't going to stop, we decided to leave.

We were later to find out that the vicar, from whom we had rented the flat, had previously had it exorcised. His method had obviously not worked.

Although I was happier in our new abode, my health was causing some concern. I had been suffering from a restriction in my throat which had not eased, and the medical profession were unable to give a diagnosis. Furthermore, my rail journey to work in London every day was becoming increasingly claustrophobic as I battled with the early morning rush.

Then one morning I noticed that someone had left a strange-looking magazine on the seat. I picked it up, and as I was idly leafing through it I realised that it was some kind of psychic journal. I thought of my paternal grandmother and of her psychic abilities, and this inspired me to look again at the classified ads. Mediums, healers, clairvoyants, tarot readers – there were so many names and telephone numbers, yet I wasn't drawn to any of them as I toyed with the idea of visiting a medium. However, on the last page of the magazine there was a notice advertising a forthcoming psychic event which was to take place at the College of Psychic Studies in London, and I felt comfortable with the idea of con-tacting them to ask for the name of a reputable medium. They were very helpful, and made an appointment for me to meet Charles Horrey, whom they assured me was an excellent medium.

Much later, I came to realise that it was no coincidence that I picked up the magazine left on the train – when the spirit world wants to tell you something, it will find a way.

When the day of my appointment arrived I was extremely nervous, but the sitting changed the course of my life. Though this encounter is fully explained in my book *Mind to Mind*, it is appropriate for what comes later for me to give a brief recap of the visit.

Charles Horrey told me that my choking was a result of exces-sive energy, and that I would continue to be ill if I did not release this energy by healing others. At the time I was perturbed by this information – who wouldn't be?

Although my mother had always asked the great healer Harry Edwards to cure all our ills, I knew nothing about the psychic world, and indeed – apart from my hand analysis studies, which

I considered to be scientific – I was not in the least bit interested. To be quite honest, being an opera fanatic filled my fantasy life quite adequately. I had never given the paranormal world a single thought, not even when my mother appeared to me. For me that was just something that 'happened' rather than part of a larger world.

As for being a healer, I had always wanted to be a vet, to heal the suffering of animals. Human beings were something else altogether. Their emotions change with the tides, and I did not feel physically capable of taking on such a daunting task.

To confuse me even further, I was told that I was already a fully-fledged medium, and that eventually my name would become a household word throughout the world. I must admit that I had to contain my laughter. I asked myself what kind of kooky world I was getting into. Then, to cap it all, the medium gave me the name of a deceased surgeon who had apparently worked at the London Hospital and who now wished to work through me.

By the time Charles Horrey had taken me through the whole of my life, giving me my mother's name and the names of other members of my family, as well as messages that no one would understand but me, I had to admit that this man *had something*. I would have to go home and think about it.

Quietly contemplating the information I had been given, my thoughts returned to the question of the mind. How could this medium possibly know all these things about me, or map out my life for the future? Was this the same force that enabled me to practise 'remote travelling'? Could he somehow project his mind in the same way? And how had he been able to communicate with my mother, who had died several years ago? It could not be because of brainpower; if it was, then we would *all* have this gift. It had to be something else. Of course, I had seen my grandmother passing on messages to the family from her deceased sons, but I was very young and really hadn't thought much about it as I was growing up. Questions invaded my mind so much now that I became more confused every moment.

There were a few hilarious moments when I returned home. Whilst explaining what had occurred during the sitting, I held up my hands and said mockingly, 'Heal, heal, I'm going to heal the world!' Suddenly, furniture began to move and loud bangs filled the house. Needless to say I stopped immediately. Something very odd indeed was happening.

Still worried about my health, I decided to test the medium's advice. If my symptoms disappeared, then I would take into account everything he had told me. If they didn't, then I would dismiss the whole episode. I was not looking forward to spending my life treating sick people. My children were grown up and I was just beginning to enjoy my own life again.

My various friends were happy to take part in the healing experiment, probably because they had so many things wrong with them. The results were amazing. One by one they were all cured of their ills, and the word soon got around that I had some kind of gift.

At the time I was working as a secretary in a local office, so the healing had to wait until the evening, but the queues of people waiting for healing (as forecast by the medium) became so long I had to give up my daytime occupation and heal full-time. I had no idea that it would lead me into the very strange world of miracles, phenomena and energy.

One of the first things I did was to buy a proper consultant's couch, covered in red leather. I had found that standing behind a patient or bending over holding their hands was extremely uncomfortable, and I can still remember the joy of the first session I spent sitting upright and relaxed. From that time on I could feel the energies flowing freely through my body and could feel the patient absorbing them.

As the weeks and months passed, all my symptoms disappeared, and I became elated by the success of the healing. It was such a joy simply looking at the people walking out of my healing room who had been so crippled on entering it that I had completely forgotten that I had only wanted to heal animals. Perhaps I was being taught a lesson? We may have our dreams, but we are not always equipped to realise them in a particular way. I know now that I would have made a lousy vet, because I am always so heartbroken when an animal has to be put to sleep. But I have found over the years that helping animals through the healing process is just as valuable – and certainly more peaceful. So perhaps my dream was realised after all.

During those early months, whilst I was still trying to come to terms with the dramatic changes in my lifestyle, questions continually invaded my mind. I felt strangely inept, out of control, dependent on the spirit world. I did not feel that I could continue with just blind faith. There had to be explanations, some sort of order – I wanted to know how it all worked.

At first I thought the healing was caused by my own magnetic energy, but that could not explain the voices that diagnosed each patient. In every case they proved to be correct. I had to admit that I was probably being helped by the surgeon who had spoken to Charles Horrey, as I could not possibly be curing these people on my own. In any event, I had never studied the physical body as I find medical journals totally unengaging.

If it *was* the spirit surgeon, then how was he able to pass the information to me? It was certainly not a brain-to-brain contact, because his had died along with the rest of his physical body. The questions never ceased.

Then one day something happened that would change my life for ever.

7

MIND ENERGY

I T HAD BEEN A VERY ORDINARY DAY, but from the moment I opened the door to my next patient it became extraordinary. Around this lady's head was an energy I had never seen before. It most definitely was not the aura one encounters surrounding the physical body, and which displays varying colours reflecting the health of the patient. This energy was pure white. But even as I ushered the lady into my healing room I sensed that the shape was wrong – it had caved in, in the middle of the head.

Whilst I was healing her, my spirit doctor gave me a diagnosis of severe depression. This was totally at odds with the symptoms she had described to me, but it made sense because the shape of the energy I could see around her head was so unlike a normal halo that the pressure on the brain must have been enormous. I was intrigued, and when I asked the patient whether she suffered from depression, she said that she did.

The whole session was fascinating. As she absorbed the healing energy the depressed halo reversed, until at the end of the session it was complete, with fingers of energy reaching out into space. As my client was leaving she told me that her depression had lifted, and that she felt happier than she had done for years.

I worried that this might be the last I would see of this incredible energy – but my spirit friends did not let me down. Throughout the whole of that day I was given the necessary clairvoyant sight and was able to study this incredible phenomenon in every patient I saw. It reacted to depressive thought by caving in, while laughter and positivity caused it to expand, and I found I could diagnose certain conditions by the small indentions in the halo.

At the end of the day it had become obvious to me that this energy had an immediate reaction to thought. I decided to call it Mind Energy.

So how did such energy link with the brain to bring about a physical reaction? We are all aware that the brain has many facets and functions, many of which are activated by thought. But I was also aware, by having read various scientific journals, that when parts of the brain are damaged or surgically removed, many patients still retain their mental faculties. Obviously, there had to be some kind of back-up, and through the actions of my friends in the spirit realms I had now been given the clairvoyant sight of that back-up.

How, I wondered, could an imbalance in this energy be reversed by healing? How could a single thought activate it, producing varying shapes in the halo? How could laughter reverse a depression? And how could one explain the energy to others? These questions and more started me on a voyage of discovery that has continued for over a quarter of a century.

The outcome of the studies I made over this period has convinced me that the mind is the control tower of the human body. By energising the brain, the mind enables it to function and send messages, via the electrically activated nervous system, to the whole body. The compartment in the brain that supposedly stores memory is only a vehicle for the mind. For it is only in the mind that every incident in our life is recorded and transferred to the Universal Mind, to be recovered whenever it is needed, and which will remain for ever in our psyche throughout many lives.

Hence the reason there are so many very young geniuses. These prodigies are able to recall knowledge they have acquired during previous lifetimes. I have heard people remark on the aptitude of such youngsters, saying that they are born geniuses. When I state that at some point during their existence, either here or elsewhere, they have had to work for that knowledge, I get some very strange looks. But that is how life works. In the end we only receive that which we are prepared to give to our progression.

My studies have also taught me that original thought does not occur in the brain, but in the mind. This is borne out by evidence from great men who, unable to solve mind-boggling problems, have fallen asleep in their laboratories, only to find on waking that they have solved the problems. I find this kind of phenomenon quite understandable, because I know that when we sleep the mind partially releases itself from the physical so that it, too, can be rejuvenated by the Universal Mind.

Sometimes, when waking from a deep sleep where the mind energy is still in an expansive state, many people have been able to see and hear spirit entities. Time and time again I have been told by patients that they have seen *me* standing by their bedside. Many of these patients were children who, in their innocence, accepted my spirit form as easily as they accepted my physical one. They have told their mothers of the conversations they had with me whilst everyone else was asleep. Unfortunately, I don't remember these journeys once my mind has returned to the physical, so I have to rely on what I am told, but I am obviously very interested to hear of my nocturnal flights. The one common factor in all the stories is that I am always seen in a long blue dress. Blue is the colour of healing, and it can often be seen as a blue mist in the healing room.

The restless mind does not like being imprisoned in the body for too long, which is why it reminds the body – via our brain – when it is time for us to rest. It is necessary for the health of both mind and body that we have a regular sleep pattern. When this is impossible our spirit flags and our health is threatened.

★   ★   ★

At the beginning of my mediumship and healing I wrote a little book called *Mind Energies and Positive Thought*. This little pocket book has been an anchor for over a million people. It reminds them that positive thought expands the halo of Mind Energy, and that negative thought depresses it. It also reminds them that by using visualisation this energy can be reversed by a single thought, and that we cannot retain guilt over our negative actions for the rest of our lives. But we can learn from these actions.

For those in normal health, the responses attained from adopting a positive outlook are immediate. The Mind Energy expands, linking into the source of healing; pressure is taken off the brain and body, and cells, tissue and organs are rejuvenated as normal circulation is restored. For people who are ill and who have debilitating diseases it takes longer and requires either hands-on healing or distant healing to give the physical body a jump-start.

The correspondence that I receive from around the world has given me positive proof that my theories are correct. It has confirmed that the replacement of negative thought with positive thought brings about a spiritual and physical change that can heal. If a complete healing cannot take place because of the degeneration of the physical body, then the disabilities will at least become less cumbersome because of the revival of the spirit. Where a healing cannot take place at all due to the complete breakdown of the physical body, healing will still give peace of mind, which in turn can relieve pain. This is because in this peace-induced state the mind partly leaves the body so that the messages from the brain to the body – i.e. the impulses that transit pain – are partially inactivated, as happens in meditation.

Again, we can see that when the brain is partially deactivated, the physical body cannot function adequately, proving that the mind *is* the control tower that governs every thought and every action and reaction in our spiritual and physical lives.

I can understand why people may be sceptical, and why a great majority of the medical profession believe that the brain governs all, because that is what they have been taught. They can demonstrate that the brain functions in different ways, stimulating nerves into action when certain parts of it are probed. What they are unable to tell us is *how* 'the brain' is stimulated so that it can react to their tests.

We know that the heart is a pump, and we also know that all major organs depend on the heart and on each other to enable the body to function correctly. But the messages for all this to happen come from the brain, and this has to have external stimulation to enable *it* to function. That external stimulation comes from the mind.

Through my extensive research into the phenomenon of Mind Energy, I have found that the easiest way to explain this power is to ask everyone to imagine a world without electricity. When the electricity is cut off, everything that depends on it is dead.

I have often seen paralysed patients get up and walk after I have worked on a Mind Energy that had somehow slipped out of sync, cutting off a vital supply of energy from the brain and body. I know hundreds of people (including myself) who have woken up to find that they are temporarily paralysed. When panic pulls the Mind Energy back into this dimension, the paralysis disappears. For a second or two it can be quite frightening, but it does prove once again that to survive in this dimension we are totally dependent on this energy.

I know it is difficult for others to understand when they do not have the clairvoyant ability to see this energy for themselves, but there are thousands of people around the world who have followed the exercises in my books and tapes and whose lives have been changed beyond recognition. They are able to heal, to be aware of spirit visitors and their messages, and their intuition has become so clear that it borders on the clairvoyant, very often expanding into the dimension of Mind Energy itself. They can gain an insight into the beauty of colour that is so dampened down in this atmosphere that we never see 'true' colours – that is a mind-changing experience of its own. And there are other factors: through my mediumistic abilities I have received thousands of messages from so-called 'dead' people. These messages have been so detailed, intimate and intelligent that the sitters themselves have been completely shocked by some of the information given about private thoughts and actions that had until that moment been their secret.

Remember, the brains of the communicators are 'dead', so they cannot be the source of information. However, Mind Energy leaves the physical body when it dies and is able to communicate by linking in with the mind of the medium. I believe that Mind Energy is the soul, the part of you that lives on for ever through many lifetimes, through many reincarnations. The point at which Mind Energy leaves the body has been seen not only by mediums but by many in the nursing profession, especially at night when the lights are low.

I have no problem with the fact that scientists and the medical profession dismiss this evidence as rubbish. After all, they have to keep in with the establishment or they will lose their status. However, although I can understand this, I cannot condone it. If they are looking for answers, then surely they should be reading about the experiences of others, especially if these same experiences are confirmed by thousands of ordinary people. These people cannot *all* be mad or weak-minded as scientists would have us believe.

I am sure that people find it as frustrating as I do when scientists talk about the brain and the mind as one, because they obviously do not know the difference between them. One will write about the *mind* doing this and that, while in a similar vein another writes about the *brain* doing the same thing. I wish they would clarify exactly which part they are talking about, as they both have different functions. The fact is, scientists are confused. Yet the majority continue to dismiss mediumistic evidence – my own clairvoyant study of Mind Energy and the incredible healing that takes place when patients are encouraged to restore their Mind Energy by positive thought.

At one time, the suggestion that mediums could see auras would be laughed at by otherwise intelligent people. Now that auras can be photographed those same people will tell you that they knew it all the time. There are so many experts who cannot wait to tell their stories *after* the event!

When I discovered Mind Energy, I described it as being pure white, although I was assured by other mediums that the energy around the head was coloured. Later that year, an American lady sent me an article cut out of a scientific journal. It was about a group of scientists who had photographed the energy around the body and head and who stated that although colours were seen around the body, the energy around the head was pure white. They could not understand why this should be so. *I* could have told them. This particular energy is spiritual, of the soul, whereas energy around the body is earth energy, which enables us to survive physically on this planet.

I have been particularly intrigued when studying the Mind Energy of people with artistic abilities. More than anyone, it seems that they can let go, allowing the mind to explore the seemingly empty space around it, expanding until the halo ceases to be defined and they are cloaked in a cloud of vapour. It is at this point that they have told me of voices and colours and of inspiration that makes them believe they have touched the hand of God. I know exactly how they feel, because without this spiritual inspiration I myself could not have written any of my books.

I have also watched Mind Energies expand and touch each other in a room full of people. Happy in conversation and in the company of associates and friends, these people have also 'let go'. This observation has helped me to understand how one mind can touch another and communicate telepathically – whether dead or alive – and to understand that this was how we received our mediumistic messages of survival.

54

This in turn led to my study of survival evidence. If my mind and the mind of the sitter mingled, was I picking up information from them rather than from someone who had died? The outcome of this study was surprising. I discovered that when a spirit person communicated through me, I could feel a tingle on the left side of my head, as well as a wonderful sensation of peace and the knowledge that I was linking into a spiritual dimension. On the other hand, when I linked with the sitter's mind, it was an entirely different experience, linking into everyday thoughts and problems. An experienced spiritual medium will stop giving evidence if she knows that she is picking up information from the client and not from a spirit entity (unless, of course, the telepathic information she's receiving will combine with the counselling she can give when the sitting ends). The best survival evidence is when the sitter does not understand the evidence at the time, but has it confirmed by another source later – it is therefore incorruptible.

I find it very strange that although good mediums can provide amazing evidence of survival, this is then shrugged off by the majority of the scientific establishment as being a simple case of telepathy, or utter rubbish. Yet it is those same people who have been telling us that telepathy doesn't exist. For those who believe it *is* telepathy, it still proves that mediums can do something that they cannot, which on their part can result in chaotic thought. But the mind *does* exist, and so does telepathy.

Wherever you go on your journey to another life, you will not be able to fool anyone as to who you really are. It will be there, on show, for everyone to see. After the death of the physical body, all is revealed. You will be shown your whole life on the screen of your mind. Every action, good or bad, and the eventual outcome of those actions will be played back to you. You will feel Heaven and Hell as you take responsibility for your actions. You will be your own judge and jury, and the monumental task of choosing a path that will redress the balance will also be of your own making. You will experience the beauty of other dimensions, and you may or may not be reincarnated to this one. But one thing is sure – everyone is given the opportunity to change. Forgiveness and progression go hand-in-hand with the love you will receive from the source of all healing.

It is sad that people pay such homage to physical beauty. If too much attention of this kind is given to a beautiful child, then the really important part of that person, the mind, can be neglected. People who do not have perfect bodies can and do have beautiful minds. They teach us how to overcome physical handicaps, they teach us how to love regardless of appearance, and they are fun to be with.

When beautiful people do not work hard mentally, they can be terribly boring. This is a pity, because if they took the time to learn, they could be both beautiful *and* interesting. Boring people are not good company and inevitably depress those who have to share their lives. And when they age they lose everything. But take heart – if you are one of these people you can change, and when you do you will rejoice when you experience what can be achieved by a truly activated mind.

The secret is to live by Universal Law. Whatever you give out will return, no matter how long it takes. It will return when you are at your lowest ebb so that it will make the maximum impact, for good or bad. Please think about this, and then learn from it.

8

TRUE SIGHT

I DID NOT REALISE, in those early days, that my vision of Mind Energy was only the beginning. I saw colours as I had only seen them before in the spiritual dimension that I had visited as a child, and later during meditation – now I could see them in all their glory, all the time. It was an unusual experience, because although it seemed that I was looking through my eyes, I knew that eyes had nothing to do with this new sight. I was actually using my mind as a third eye, and it felt so right, and natural.

Then a spirit mentor showed me an x-ray version of the physical body and gave me a lecture on the energy system, including meridian lines, chakras, and the energy link between brain and mind. Everything was pulsating, vibrating, and I could see not only the parts of the energy system that were blocked but how, when I placed my hands on the blockage, it simply dispersed.

This experience led me to think that I might be able to use this x-ray method to diagnose problems in the physical body, but unfortunately it was not to be. My talents did not work in that way. I certainly did not want to study medical journals because I found them too depressing – always giving the cause and probable medication but practically no information about prevention. Fortunately, there was another way of treating my patients. My spirit mentor continued to assist me, and he gave me a guided tour of the system and explicit instructions about how to use my mind to clear blockages and diagnose problems in the energy system.

From the time I first saw Mind Energy, something extraordinary had happened to me. I had no idea what it was at first, but it later became clear that the vibration in the Mind Energy had altered so that I could easily see through physical matter to attend to the unique energy system that sustains us.

Later, I was taught how to operate on the energy system, and you can read about this in my third book, *Mind Waves*. This ability has never left me and I use it in a hundred different ways every day of my life. I find it especially useful when I am giving distant healing and need to know more about the condition of the patient. I simply think of them, and am given an image from which I can make a diagnosis.

When an animal is involved I also use telepathy, because of the creature's disadvantage at not being able to communicate in our language. Sometimes, when an owner has a telepathic link with their pet, they still like to have their diagnosis confirmed. Through x-ray vision I have been able to cure many animals that were diagnosed as incurable by their veterinary surgeons. Because animals are naturally psychic, the telepathic communication can be an eye-opener. It can also be extremely funny when I pick up what the animals really think of the people they are living with!

I think it is important for people to realise that we have this alternative sight and sound. It has probably never occurred to most people that the mind, although separate from the physical body, is the powerhouse that drives the computer (i.e. the brain), which in turn activates the physical. Then again, why should it occur to them? As long as the physical body obeys all the commands and they are healthy, who cares? The only time we worry is when something goes wrong, when the body is receiving distorted messages from the brain and creating havoc. This closes the meridian lines, through which our life force flows, causing blockages which alter the vibrational rate of our major organs – and so the disruption goes on through the system. But the mind comes into its own when brain damage has occurred. Unable to communicate directly with ordinary people, it releases itself from the physical and moves around in the spiritual dimension, searching for someone like myself who can receive and pass on messages to family and friends – as in the case of Bobby Keetch in the first chapter of this book.

It would be impossible for me to remember all the mind-to-mind contacts I have received in this manner, but it would certainly be in the thousands. Whenever I receive a letter asking for help, the mind contact is immediate, and the healing begins.

This is my seventh book, and in all my books I have tried to teach my readers how to expand their Mind Energy so that they can at least enhance their intuition. Intuition is the first level of clairvoyance (which incidentally means clear sight), so please pause at this point, and follow my instructions.

> Choose a quiet spot, and sitting on an upright chair, fix your eyes on a blank spot on the wall and visualise a halo. If your power of visualisation is good then you can also conjure up a face beneath it. If not, keep the image simple. If you have no visualisation talent at all, just *know* that it is there, and your thought processes will do the rest.
>
> Now, with the power of your mind, expand the halo and know that it is reaching out to join the Universal Mind. Put as little emphasis behind the thought as possible, for too much effort can actually close the mind.

When you have read these instructions and know them by heart, you can practise every day. You may find it easier to visualise if you close your eyes. You will find that latent talents come to the fore, and you will become more intuitive, more attuned to the feelings of others.

If you are successful and would like to follow this up with meditation, anything can happen. You will certainly see colour in a new light. Friends and relatives who have died can show themselves to you. It all depends on how much you really *want* to see, how dedicated you are. I can assure you that your efforts will be rewarded in many different ways.

9

THE UNIVERSES

IT HAD BEEN A TYPICAL summer's day in 1976. When night came I decided to sit in the garden and look at the night sky, a favourite occupation of mine. I was not particularly interested in the formation of the stars, only the need to go beyond the visible, to peep behind the curtains of energy that blind our vision.

When I was evacuated during the Second World War, the people to whom my welfare had been entrusted locked me out of the house from dusk to dark whilst they visited friends or went to the local cinema. I was ten years old, afraid of the dark, and alone. Near the house was a tall conifer tree which had a small opening in the side through which I crawled and climbed to the top. It was my secret place.

Looking at the night sky became something that I enjoyed very much. I felt that somewhere in that vast space there was a place called home. I instinctively knew that I had come from somewhere 'out there' and that one day I would return.

So it did not come as a complete surprise to me when, in 1976, I was given a vision of not one Universe but a multitude of Universes, and I was given the knowledge that these Universes were not a million miles away but were hidden between folds of energy structures that were so different to our own system as to make them invisible to humans.

I had known for many years that our eyes, compared with mind vision, were like little portholes which could see only that which exists in our immediate vicinity. With particularly good eyesight it might be possible to see a distant landscape quite clearly, but that is all. We are so limited, in fact, that it is impossible to describe that limitation unless one can accept the concept of an infinite mind.

All my life I have been able to see beyond this dimension. I have also been able to hear voices giving me advice or, in the face of danger, 'commands'. I have always been aware that I am never truly alone, that someone is always there for me. This has not made my life any easier as one is expected to put in a hundred per cent before being helped over the most difficult hurdles. Some of the decisions I have made during my life have been as stupid as the next person's, but every time I made a mistake, or unwittingly harmed someone, I was taught a valuable lesson. There is no escape from Universal Law, which determines that whatever one gives out, good or bad, will return when one is at one's lowest ebb, for the optimum impact. This does not only apply to what you have done in *this* life. The mind is everlasting, so whatever is left over from a previous life will still count. Hopefully, in time, our intuition will become strong enough for us to heed the advice we are being given through our senses – only then will our decisions become wiser.

Whilst living in this particular dimension, we have somehow to learn the art of balance. We are presumably not here to become Holier than Thou, or give up our earthly pleasures, but we must try to balance the odds of having to face up to our own demeanours when we leave this Earth. It's rather like facing your parents with poor exam results. The words, '*God, what have I done now?*' have played a major role in my life and, I suspect, that of everyone who inhabits the same place at this time.

With this knowledge already in my psyche, I was not unduly puzzled when the plethora of Universes were shown to me. When the vision began, I was neither meditating nor asleep, but wide awake looking up at the night sky. It was as though giant slides were being slipped into place, each one bearing a different picture to the last. Even the stars were different. On some slides the stars constantly changed shape – some oval, some round, some elliptical – while others danced around like free spirits. Sometimes I seemed to be looking at a plain jet black canvas with a light behind it, as though it was blocking out the vision of a much brighter galaxy.

Then something extraordinary happened. I found that I had been enveloped in an energy that was soft, almost fluid, and that I was at the centre of these unfolding pictures. I had an image of myself in a transparent bubble, surrounded by larger bubbles which were endlessly rotating in their own atmospheres, constantly over-lapping at the edges as though the spheres were catching up on time. Then something gently placed me back in my chair in the garden, as though I were a precious porcelain doll. I have never before or since felt such love and tenderness as I did that night.

The experience was so special that for a long time I could not speak of it to anyone. But from that day on I told anyone who might be interested that the Universe we inhabit is much smaller than we imagine, and that there are Universes so expansive that they defy description.

I am sure that a physicist could explain my experience better than I, but I do not have their expertise and, as far as I know, no one else has had the same experience. One day, perhaps, it may plant a seed in a scientifically/spiritually-oriented mind and open up a door to the secrets of the Universes. I know that scientists are constantly vying for the big ego-boosting prizes available to them when a great discovery has been made. Over the years, several scientists have picked my brain for ideas that might enhance their reputation. But for me no prize could be greater than the sum of my incredible experiences over so many years. They are the greatest gifts of all.

I also know that if scientists do not become spiritually

orientated, then they will never discover the secrets of these multiple Universes. To see them, to experience the sensation, one has to leave behind the notion that the brain is the governing factor in our lives. They must accept the mind for what it is, a spiritual gift that governs the whole. Then, with the mind, they will really be able to 'see' for the first time and they will find that the earthly prizes they have been striving for do not matter. They will be given experiences that will change their lives and those of the people around them – and that, perhaps, will change the world.

I do not have their scientific talents, and they do not have mine. But they could listen and learn from me. It would be an incredible stepping stone in mankind's search for Universal answers.

10

A WHOLE BAG OF TOOLS

IN CHAPTER 8 I MENTIONED how I was taught by my spirit
surgeons to give psychic surgery on the body's energy counterpart. I am aware how difficult it must be for people to accept that
something like this could happen, but all healing is dependent on
the entities who attach themselves to the healer's mind, enabling
them to use their particular talents coupled with the healer's own
personality and intelligence. It is always a meeting of two minds.
Sometimes, several entities are in attendance and, because I am a
medium, I have been able to listen to their remarks as they give
their diagnosis. However, although I was impressed with the
results of the operations, I realised that I could not treat everyone
who needed this type of healing, so I decided to experiment to
find out whether I could discover a way of teaching others how
to treat themselves with the 'tools of the trade'.

I set about building a pharmacy and healing room with my
mind. The first step was to visualise an empty room with two
huge windows, as I am addicted to light. When the room was
suddenly flooded with sunlight, I knew that I was not alone and
was being guided along this path, which would eventually enable
everyone to become adept at healing themselves. From that point
my task became easier as I filled the walls with cupboards and
added work-tops to the dozens of drawers that had grown up

from the floor as if by magic. A steel sink and drainer were installed under the window. The first part of the exercise was complete. Now it was time to fill the cupboards and drawers with varying sizes of empty bottles, phials, syringes, cotton wool, and other bits and pieces that I thought I might need. I imbued the walls and ceiling with a pale blue, which is the colour of healing energy, then added a huge cosy armchair and a small stool. Whilst I was trying the imaginary armchair out for size and comfort, I felt someone place their hands on my shoulders.

When I awoke I realised that I had been 'away' for an hour. The spirit healing had come as a complete surprise, because I had intended that this room would be for self-healing, for taking over the responsibility for one's own health. And yet, once again, I was being shown that it could also be a place where one could ask for help, and that in this room – in our mind space – anything goes. I decided to leave the next step to the following day, and wondered whether my next visit would mean having to rebuild an empty room, or whether it would remain as I had left it.

Because of previous commitments I did not go back into my medicine room for another three days, and I was very apprehensive when I opened the door of my mind so that I could enter. I suppose I should have had more faith in the process, for the room was just as I had left it. It was time for the next step. I visualised a box of self-adhesive labels and a pen, and began to write. After a while every bottle was labelled, and the contents of every drawer were listed. I was now ready to teach others how to manage their health problems.

I must point out that whatever one *thinks* the bottles contain, it will be so. The mind can reproduce any substance in energy, which is transferred through the energy system and then manifests in the physical. But do not dwell on this explanation, because too much thought can be tiring and will, consequently, close the mind. Just treat yourself as you think fit, and then forget it; your mind will do the rest. The less impact that goes into the thought, the more powerful the treatment will be.

When I felt that I had thought of everything I left the room and, as I locked the door I felt as though I was on the threshold of a new and exciting period in my healing work.

For the next two months I visited this room every day, treating myself for several small problems and even giving myself a beauty treatment. I certainly felt better in myself, and believed that I would be able to tend my own minor medical needs. To my spiritual requests for hands-on healing, the response was immediate, enabling me to work longer hours whenever necessary. There was no doubt in my mind that this form of self-healing was working, and I called my special mind space 'The Mind Medicine Room'.

I then decided that if I was to move on with this experiment, I had to involve my patients, preferably those with no psychic ability. My first pupils were two women and one man whom I knew were addicted to dependency. I wanted them to savour the freedom of independence from others, to be able to make their own instruments, to fill the cupboards and drawers in their own Mind Medicine Rooms with every conceivable type of medical equipment they felt they might need, now and in the future. They would, for the first time in their lives, be able to make their own decisions without having to involve others. I went to great lengths to point out that this sort of treatment was only for minor ailments or to supplement medical treatments for more serious problems, and that it formed a part of the whole healing, physical and spiritual. The most difficult part of the experiment was trying to teach them how to visualise, because for some reason they thought visualisation was a special psychic ability. But when I asked them to close their eyes and picture a bag of cotton wool balls, they did so with ease. I then asked them to watch the cotton wool turning red; the male patient found this difficult until I told him to 'know' that it had turned red. He found the 'knowing' factor easier than actually trying to 'see' a picture. Then I asked them to turn some of the cotton wool balls pink, and to gradually see the colour darkening by degrees until it was red. After only a few teaching sessions they were all able to do this with ease.

One day, one of the women arrived with a bandage on her left leg. She told me that she had fallen over and received a deep flesh wound which had been attended to by her doctor. I used this opportunity to teach the other two pupils how to take the victim of the accident into their healing rooms and to heal her, whilst she remained in her own room and healed herself. I told them to take the cotton wool out of the bag, place it on the wound on their friend's leg, and watch as it gradually turned from pink to red, knowing that as it did so it was drawing out inflammation and any bacteria that might have invaded it. Then I told them to remove the red cotton wool, replace it with a new piece, and go through the whole process again until they stopped 'seeing' or 'knowing' the cotton wool change colour. In this kind of healing there is always a time limit for the mind. To finish, I asked them to take a small bottle of antibiotic fluid out of a drawer and to dab the fluid on the wound, which they were then to cover with a bandage. I reminded them that they had to go through this process every day until they returned the following week for another lesson. They were all delighted when the patient phoned them the following day to say that the wound on her leg had completely disappeared. Needless to say, they were eager to carry out more difficult tasks.

Every week I taught them something different until they could, with ease, give insulin injections to imaginary patients, give themselves antacid tablets whenever they had heartburn or tablets to prevent the recurrence of acid problems. One of the women had suffered with dandruff for many years, so she washed her hair every day with an anti-dandruff lotion, and within two weeks the dandruff had disappeared. My three pupils were beginning to get results and, as they did so they found a confidence and independence that none of them in their wildest dreams had thought they could realise. They had freed their Mind Energy and, in return, it had shown them the secret of life itself. Their lives changed completely, and they were no longer dependent on others for their happiness – they were now complete human beings.

From these first pupils I went on to teach thousands of patients the methods I had used with them, and I made a tape to help people set up their own 'Mind Medicine Room'. I hope this chapter will inspire thousands more to become responsible for their own health and happiness, and perhaps to help others when they are in need. This way you can teach your body how it should be working *for* you rather than against you.

On studying the energies of my pupils, from the first lesson to the last, I noticed that the Mind Energy did not react at all whilst they were struggling, which told me that they had not yet reached the state of consciousness which involves Mind Energy, that they were still in the lower imaginative state which is based mainly on brain function. It was immediately apparent when the Universal consciousness was reached, not only to me but to them; they described it as the 'dream state', which was in fact an apt description of what it feels like when the mind momentarily leaves the physical body and produces images from the mind dimension. This shows in the PET scans that are carried out whilst people are dreaming, when the de-energised brain produces very little activity; the brain only shows itself to be fully active when the mind returns and energises it when we are awake. Most scientists involved in the experiments on the 'dream state' fail to see the incredible and indelible truth in their results.

If you want to try the 'Mind Medicine Room' for yourself, do remember that there are vast numbers of people who cannot visualise and cannot 'see' colours. If you are one of these people, I can assure you that by simply 'knowing' that whatever you are thinking is really happening, you will be successful. The only thing that *could* affect the outcome is if you have any doubt at all that you can do it. Doubt will close down all the energy channels, so you must get rid of any negative thoughts about your ability to carry out the exercises that you set yourself.

If anyone reading this is addicted to drugs, smoking or alcohol, you can visit your room, sit in the chair, and mentally indulge yourself. You will find that your physical addiction will lessen over time and peace will enter your heart and mind. Why not try it? There is nothing to lose, and everything to gain.

Those who are successful will find their talents particularly suited to giving distant healing anywhere in the world. I know, because I have had a million or more letters to prove it.

11

MEDITATION

SOARING ABOVE THE MOUNTAINS AT SUNSET, arms outstretched like a great eagle surveying its territory, I found myself drawn toward a golden globe of light. It swung to and fro in the light breeze as though suspended from an invisible thread. Intrigued, I moved closer, and as I did so I was engulfed in a dazzling white light. I felt myself spinning, my inner peace replaced with a feeling of 'knowing' as I reached my destination. I had been here before – long ago.

The herb garden in which I was standing was so familiar I knew exactly where each herb had been planted. Walking down an old brick path, I bent down to pick sprigs of lavender, crushing them between my fingers. Cupping the leaves in my hands, I held them to my face and inhaled their perfume. Images from another age passed through my mind as I savoured the sight and smells of sage, peppermint, rosemary, thyme, and lemon verbena.

It was then I saw him. His frock coat swung as he turned to look at me, blue eyes shining through small silver spectacles. The sun shone on his shoulder-length hair as he walked toward me. He held out his hands in greeting, and said, 'We are the same person, you and I, but I am sure you know that.'

I had seen this man many times whilst giving trance healings, and also whilst meditating. I had guessed that he was a doctor and that he had been a herbalist, as I had seen him making herbal potions before visiting his patients in his pony and trap. I had no idea who he was or why I was being given these pictures, but I always felt peaceful whenever I was in his presence. I also knew instinctively that he was one of the doctors helping me in my healing practice. Now I was enthralled. I had inadvertently opened a door in my mind space that had enabled me to return to a previous life. At least I had solved one mystery. But why was I here, at this moment?

We talked for some time, the doctor and I, and I asked him how it was that we could both exist at the same time in different time sequences. His eyes seemed to look straight through me as he said, 'We always leave a little bit of ourselves behind whenever we move on.' Then a mischievous smile lit his face and, lightly touching my face with his hand, he said, 'Of course, some would say that I am only an illusion.' He chuckled, turned, and walked away without a backward glance. I have never seen him again. Although he had polished yet another facet of the mediumistic diamond for me, he had also been true to form with all my experiences with my spirit teachers: he had left me with a difficult task – to fathom the secret of time.

When I finally returned to my healing room where I had been meditating, I knew that my life would never be the same again. His words had convinced me that whatever we have been, we continue to be. That the mind is for ever.

Meditation is, and in retrospect has always been, part of my daily ritual. Throughout my childhood my family always called me a 'daydreamer'. What they did not know, and I do not think they would have understood, was the incredible journeys I used to take into other worlds. Even if they had been aware of these journeys they would have dismissed them as childish fantasies. But I kept them to myself; they were my secret worlds, places where I would meet people who guided me through strange landscapes, explaining as they walked beside me the significance of what we were seeing and what we were about to see as we peered through the mists into the unknown. The most interesting part of these excursions was the expectation; the most magical were the brightly coloured birds and flowers. Time and again, I was told that cruelty to any living creature was against all spiritual laws. Sometimes I was taken to a place where we sat and listened in silence. I did not hear any words, but as an adult I came to realise that I had been picking up the information telepathically.

When I returned to our world, I remembered in detail the visions of those other worlds, but I was too young to interpret what I had seen and heard. Perhaps the lessons were meant to be retained in my psyche until it was time to bring them to the surface again.

I suppose a psychiatrist would say that I disappeared into a fantasy world because I was unhappy. Not true. All this happened before I was evacuated at the tender age of ten. Until that time I had been extremely happy, part of a very loving, extended family. My mother, her sister and friends were all members of the Church of England; my aunt was a Sunday School teacher and head of the local church's Brownie pack; my paternal grandmother was a medium and an ardent Spiritualist. My mother was afraid of mediums, so one can only guess at the relationship she had with my grandmother, but later in her life she was to become a great supporter of Harry Edwards, the famous healer. I have often remarked to friends when telling them about my first mediumistic encounter – the time my mother came through and told me that I was going to be a great healer – that if she had anything to do with my future she would probably try to turn me into another Harry Edwards. She must have found a way to overcome her fear of mediums, and I still think she had a lot to do with what I have become.

So was it the church that inspired my visions? Certainly not! Because what I saw was totally different to anything I had been taught, and the pictures and stories in the many religious books I read were nothing like my adventures.

The thing I hated most about the church was always having to look at Jesus on the Cross. I could actually feel the pain of the nails that had been driven through his flesh. I do not believe this was fanciful either, because as a healer one never stops feeling the pain of others. Also, having to walk around the church on Good Friday, stopping at the Stations of the Cross for what seemed like hours, until we reached the crucifixion, was a totally negative experience for one so young. It was at these times that I wished I could visit my other worlds, where peace, serenity and love reigned. But I could not do this until I had forgotten the pain of the crucifixion. I believed then, and I believe now, that it is not an appropriate sight for small children. In this day and age, where murder, violence and all sorts of unspeakable crimes are to be seen daily on our television sets, we do not need to see yet more visions of violence whilst visiting a place of worship. We need peace, our children need peace, and it is time our churches gave it to us.

It is time also for preachers to speak less of the Devil and all His works and teach the power of healing. This would be a step in the right direction. If one's mind becomes fixed on a disturbing image in childhood and continues into adult life, the mind can create disturbing physical symptoms, even stigmata.

Since I became a medium and healer, I have often thought about my childhood visions, and I now believe that they were part of the psychic talent inherited from my paternal grandmother. This obviously overwhelmed anything I was being taught by my mother, even though I was with her every day and only saw my grandmother on Sundays. I was a born medium and healer. Another reason for this belief is that when I was evacuated during the war I was for the first time in my life unloved, ignored and practically starved. Although my need to visit my other worlds became greater than ever, the ability to do so had gone. I felt that

I had been deserted by everyone, until eventually the spirits visited me in my bedroom. I knew then that they would never let me down.

I wish I had known then about the ability of the mind to leave the body, to be free. At least I would have understood that whatever problems we have in our lives, no one can damage or destroy the perfect gift that we have all been given – the gift of the mind. I would also have understood that when we become overwhelmed by the stresses of everyday problems we are imprisoning our mind, the one energy that has the ability to leave, refuel and return to the physical to re-energise our brain and body. Finally, I would have realised that we can overcome most of our normal problems by regular meditation.

Over the years I have been privy to the intimate details of thousands of people's lives. Whenever I have introduced the idea of meditation, most people have told me that they could not possibly do that because they do not have any psychic ability. So I ask them just to close their eyes and picture their children, a happy holiday they have enjoyed, or a room in their home – anything, as long as it is simple. They laugh when they find how easy it is to visualise such things. Some people have complained that the pictures are not in colour, others that they know the picture is there but cannot see any details; but most have managed to see *something*. They also realise that by picturing one of their children, they can *feel* the child's emotions, or become aware that something's been happening they were not conscious of before visiting me. I always ask them to check these details, and they usually tell me later that they found that they had indeed locked into something that had given them instant information.

This experience has intrigued so many people that they have asked me to show them how to meditate. So I've introduced them to 'daydreaming' and extended it, little by little, to deep meditation, where we let go of the mind and allow it to travel and bring back images and information. It's the first time people become aware that the brain and mind are different and separate, but that we need both to be able to function adequately in this dimension.

Meditation is the best anti-stress treatment imaginable – and it is free! Simply sit down in a quiet room and daydream. The first stage is to take yourself back to your childhood and think of all the happy times you experienced as part of a family. If your childhood was unhappy, simply go forward to a time when you were content. Once you have slipped into a deep daydreaming mode, you will be surprised by how many memories which you thought you had forgotten come to the fore. Remember, you are opening doors of the mind that have been closed for a long time. Sink deeper into the daydreaming mode, and 'let go'. At this point you may fall asleep.

When you try daydreaming again, go through the first step as before, and then open the doors to your life at different ages. The same thing will happen; happy memories locked away for years will emerge, and you will find yourself smiling. If you do not fall asleep at this point, think of the future and what you wish it to be. You will find that the pictures will take on a life of their own. You will be given ideas to help you build a happy future and to avoid the pitfalls of the past.

When you have got to this stage, relax completely, and you will automatically experience the full meditation process. It actually sounds easier than it is, so please don't give up if it takes time to master. Keep going, and in a few weeks you will be on your way. I have only one warning: if you recall any unpleasant memories, put them into your mental dustbin and throw them away. They are not only negative but also useless material taking up valuable space in your mind. Never allow that to happen again, whether you are fully awake or meditating. You are the only person who can make things happen for you, things that can bring happiness into your life. Relying on others to do this for you will result in chaos, because human beings are just – well, human – people who may at some time let you down.

I have had so many incredible experiences in a lifetime of meditation. The following are examples of some of my own meditations and the way in which our minds touch the Universal Mind, and we can all learn from this.

I found myself floating through endless corridors. The walls, ceiling and floors were white marble and, without touching them, I could feel their texture and temperature. I was expecting them to feel cold, but they were so warm that I was reminded of when, as a child, I warmed my hands in front of the coal fire on frosty winter days. I thought of my mother, and longed to be with her once more, to feel the warmth of her body and the love that she so willingly gave throughout her life. It seemed as if I was being given pictorial accounts of the love I had received. These pictures went on and on. When they had finished, and I eventually reached the end of the corridor, I could see my mother standing there, waiting for me. I reached out for her, but as I got closer she backed away, holding her hands up in the air as though to stop my progress, and I knew that she was telling me that although she could help me from a distance, I was on my own. I heard her say, 'You have so much to give. There are others waiting to teach you.' And then she disappeared.

This meditation experience happened at the time when I was at the very beginning of my mediumship and healing. It had such an impact on me that when I opened my eyes I could not believe I was still sitting in my own home.

The following meditation brought me into contact with hundreds of animals.

It was as though I had been transported to a planet filled with nothing but animals. I walked among lions, tigers, elephants, horses, giraffes, as well as cats and dogs, all peacefully sharing the same space. There were so many species, and many that I could not identify. I was in my element. The animals and I were telepathically connected, and I could feel the pain and despair that they had suffered at some time in their eternal lives.

The strange thing about this experience was the fact that I felt as though I had come to *them* for healing and not the reverse, that the love and care that emanated from these creatures was the same as that experienced during the natural healing process. The minds of all living things are interconnected, and telepathy is the only way through the mess that human beings have made of their world. It is the only way to completely understand each other, because we have complicated our lives with hundreds of different languages, which form a permanent barrier to resolving most of the terrible tragedies that are being played out every day around the world.

And I had been taught this, not by some great philosopher or guru, but by the love that had evolved from great suffering – from the animals.

I found myself standing on the top of a hill, looking down into a valley filled with flowers. There were hundreds of different species of all shapes and sizes, and the colours – as always – were brilliant because there was no pollution contaminating the atmosphere.

Then, without any sensation of having moved away from the hill, I realised that I was actually standing in the middle of this vast ocean of flowers. The perfume was quite amazing, a reminder of the old-fashioned roses that used to grow in abundance in cottage gardens.

Without warning, I then found myself surrounded by thousands of poppies, which once again triggered distant memories from my childhood. I was shown hedgerows full of birds' nests, and the birdsong in these areas was beautiful. I was then shown birds that have ceased to exist in our dimension.

The experience continued until I had seen every form of nature that has been affected by the disastrous things we have done to our environment. The beauty and joy I had felt at the beginning of the meditation now turned to a deep sorrow and to the realisation that we must return to a natural organic process.

There was no doubt in my mind when I came out of the meditation that a dire warning had been contained in this experience. Millions of ordinary people in this world have been aware of the dangers of using poisonous chemicals on the land for the past fifty years or so. But their voices have not been heeded. If they had been, agricultural pharmacists and industrialists would have had to take a massive cut in profits. Consequently, not only has the land been poisoned to such an extent that it is bereft of natural elements that are essential to our health, such as selenium, but the animals and birds who live on the land are so affected that many species are now endangered, while thousands have already died.

Human beings are also affected. Even if the practice of poisoning our soil was stopped today, we would still be ingesting the chemicals through the food chain a hundred years from now. (There will be more on this towards the end of the book in the chapter 'The Planet in Peril'.)

I have received many warnings through my meditations, and those I received twenty-five years ago are being played out now. That is why I believe the warnings to be thought transference from the minds of those outside our environment, those who can see the whole picture.

12

CHANGE CAN ONLY HAPPEN WHEN THE SPIRIT SOARS

KIRAN BEDI IS A REMARKABLE WOMAN. Her spirituality gave her the courage to stand alone and to bring about positive changes in the lives of thousands of people. I would like to thank my friends Sharon Baylis and Michael Bott for sharing this story with me, and for allowing me to share it with you. It is an inspiration to us all.

Tihar Jail in New Delhi is the size of a small town. It was designed to hold three thousand people. Instead, it holds ten thousand men, women and children. The desolation of the surroundings reflects the dire poverty of the inmates. There are no means of occupation, education or recreation, and the prison is a breeding ground for the very crimes it was designed to punish. Drugs are endemic, prostitution flourishes, corruption breeds, and violence and fear lurk in every corner. Remand prisoners, including women with their children, can languish here for up to ten years before their cases come to trial, sharing overcrowded cells with petty thieves, murderers and addicts. Under a succession of male governors, mob management barely maintains the status quo, and the problems are more than the staff can handle. Inmates are sometimes shot at random by prison officers out of control.

That was in 1993. Twenty years before, Kiran Bedi was a small, boyish and bright-eyed tennis star who abandoned the sporting jet set to become the first female officer in the Indian police force. In India, a woman's place is *not* in a position of authority. Although she rose swiftly through the ranks, Bedi was a thorn in the side of the male establishment. Appointing her as governor to Tihar was just one more attempt to demoralise and sideline her; her ignominious failure was considered inevitable. So it was that in July 1993 this extraordinary woman stepped into the bubbling cauldron of Tihar Jail.

But within months of her appointment, Bedi had turned Tihar around. She fired the worst prison officers, then began a radical restructure of the prisoners' day. She introduced a complaint box for inmates to air their grievances. She initiated drug rehabilitation, health care, yoga therapy, prayer meetings, music, arts and crafts sessions, adult literacy and physical fitness programmes. Idleness was banished, every hour of the day was positively accounted for, and she achieved this by motivation and encouragement, not by the 'compelling force of law'.

Bedi's philosophy is simple yet profound.

The philosophy is to provide them with a positive environment in which they have opportunities to correct the thought processes, to bring in time management to themselves . . . an environment in which they redevelop respect for society and authority. They redevelop compassion for each other, they somehow lessen the feelings of vengeance and revenge, and learn that these are literally the things that have led them there – and how to control them. This is what I think the philosophy should be and this is what we're trying to do for them.

To men and women used to the rule of the stick and the gun, the arrival of Kiran Bedi was like a gift from the Gods. Nine months into her tenure, Bedi began her most radical innovation – introducing inmates to the Vispana system of meditation.

> I was looking for a magic. I've been calling Vispana a magic therapy. I was looking for a real behaviour-change therapy. Not just listening and then forgetting it after two days, but something which they could listen to and actually practise as they go through an experience of behavioural change themselves.

Bedi astonished and outraged the authorities by inviting to Tihar the world-renowned meditation guru S. N. Goenka.

> I think he is one of the most learned teachers I have ever come across ... I see him as a living Buddha, a living saint, and the country is very lucky that it has a teacher like him. He is very precious to this country.

One thousand prisoners, ten per cent of Tihar's population, took part in the largest meditation experiment in the history of the world's prisons, spending ten hours a day meditating and listening to spiritual instruction. The idea was to free the mind, even behind locked doors. For the prisoners, the experience was nothing short of miraculous. The changes wrought by the experiment were equally miraculous – discipline improved, medical problems declined; Tihar became cleaner, healthier, more settled, more peaceful.

The authorities who appointed Kiran Bedi in the expectation of destroying her saw her turn every obstacle to her advantage, winning the trust, respect – and love – of both prisoners and officers. She was given the Magsaysay award for public service, and although her time at Tihar was short-lived, the changes she instituted have had a lasting effect. Prisoners who leave the jail do not usually return.

★   ★   ★

This story also intrigued me for another reason. Since the publication of my books, I have been receiving letters from the inmates of prisons from all over the country. One of the main problems prisoners describe is the terrible feeling of claustrophobia they experience when they are locked in their cells – lack of air, lack of daylight, and hundreds of wasted hours.

One of the first things I taught them was how to 'let go' and daydream, an easy introduction to the art of meditating. I then taught them the basics of *mind power*, the incredible feats of the infinite mind and about spirituality. They took to it because it was nothing to do with religion but was the way in which we, as individuals, could strengthen and shape our Mind Energy and link in with the Universal Mind.

I also taught prisoners the basics of Universal Law, that whatever you give out *will* return at some time or another, and that to ensure a happy, healthy and productive life you have to give out all that you would wish to happen in your own life: if you give out evil, evil will return; if you give good, it will return; and if you give compassion, so it will return.

The most difficult lesson for them to learn was taking 'responsibility for self'. Some of the letters I received on this subject were hilarious. It seemed that every wrong-doing they had committed had been the fault of someone else. They were adamant that had they been born in different circumstances, they would not have been in the predicament in which they now found themselves. I believe that I did manage to get through to some of them, but I don't know how many finished their jail sentences still in this frame of mind. I argued that there were many prisoners who had been born with all the advantages of wealth and that this still had not prevented them from becoming criminals.

Those who had genuinely been wrongly imprisoned found the meditation techniques invaluable as they fought for their freedom, and once outside they have continued with this regime. They told me that it was only their daily meditation sessions – which had eventually enabled them to partially leave the body and visit their loved ones – that had saved their sanity.

It was a fascinating exercise teaching the inmates about the survival of the mind. Very few were sceptical, and practically all of them believed that there was life after death. Their belief had not come from any religious source but from stories that had been handed down through the ages by family members. Many had seen ghosts and the spirit forms of relatives when they had been under great stress. I was able to explain to them that stress does cause Mind Energy to expand and that the same happens when people go into shock, for example in an accident. When this happens, the mind is able to see into other dimensions – it becomes, in fact, our third eye.

If only our prison governors would take a leaf out of Kiran Bedi's book – or my own, for that matter. They would then perhaps be able to boast that twenty per cent of the prisoners released would be a credit to our society. Prisoners serving long sentences could form small meditation groups, taught whenever possible by experienced teachers.

If I were a governor, I would be ashamed to think that a woman who was totally opposed by her colleagues and the system could turn around the most terrible prison in India and yet, with conditions in this country ninety per cent better, and with masses of aid, they cannot do it here.

From what I can gather from the letters I receive from inmates who have been incarcerated for years, one of their worst fears is the terror they experience at the hands of small groups of thugs. By the time they are released they have become mental and physical wrecks. In this state they are naturally incapable of finding work, and once again the country has to support them, albeit in a different way. If they and the thugs had been introduced to meditation and to the expansion of the mind, they would have been whole human beings by the time they were ready to leave prison. As whole human beings, they would be a credit to society.

Instead, we are faced with looking after broken bodies and minds which are incapable of thinking *straight*, and so along the crooked road they go, because they have not been shown a different way.

This has to change, and Kiran Bedi had the answer. For anyone reading this chapter who can bring about change in prisons, please read her story again and again, and then do something about it.

13

FEAR

WHAT HAPPENS WHEN FEAR becomes your bedfellow? In this day and age, the fear of being attacked and mugged is with us all. But there is another kind of fear, one that causes people to forget about their principles, their morals, and to cause unnecessary hardship to others. This is the fear of not being accepted as part of the Establishment. The governing bodies in this country have drawn up so many rules that even their members are not sure when they are breaking them. Most people are either unaware or could not care less about these established bodies, and it was only when I became a medium and healer that I became interested, because I was involved in many of their petty attitudes.

I will give you some examples. I had a patient who, because of the disintegration of the vertebrae in her spine, had to be carried up the steps of my home and into my healing room. She had been in a wheelchair for years, and had completely given up hope. Gradually, over many months, the healing energy rebuilt her spine until it was healthy once again. The life of this very courageous lady returned to normal and she found that she could run up and down the steps to my home where she had once had to crawl.

When she went for her usual check-up at the hospital, she took along her old x-rays and asked for new ones to be taken. This was done. When the specialist looked at the new films and compared them with the old, he simply would not accept that they had been taken of the same spine, and told my patient flatly that her previous x-rays belonged to someone else. 'But I've been in a wheelchair for years!' she exclaimed. 'How can you say that?' The specialist would not budge, and eventually passed her on to a colleague rather than admit that she had had a miracle cure.

I was amazed when she told me this story. I would have thought that her specialist would have been delighted at the outcome. But over the years, this type of reaction never alters. Instead of doctors being happy with their patients' eventual recovery, they simply dismiss their stories.

Another case was that of a young man who was being given psychiatric help once a month. He was very distressed when he visited me for the first time, because he was frightened of the doctor who was treating him. 'I know I've got worse since I started sessions with him,' he said. 'Please help me.' His was a simple case of stress, nothing serious, and yet he felt that the psychiatrist was treating him more and more like a mental case. After only four healing sessions with me he was back to normal, had found a new job and a new life, and was extremely happy. He wanted to tell his psychiatrist about his new-found happiness and duly made an appointment to visit him. When he told his story, the psychiatrist told him to get out and never return. He simply did not want to know about the young man's recovery and subsequent happiness. My patient returned to me utterly devastated by the way he had been treated. His remark was, 'They only want to see the unhappiness in your life.' Over the years I am afraid that I have found this largely to be true.

Literally thousands of people who have been cured of their ailments and who have had the courage to speak to their specialist or GP about it have had to put up with the most appalling insults. I can understand how overworked doctors are and, although this is no excuse for their bad manners, I can relate to their frustration when a patient talks about a form of healing they know nothing about. But it is the doctors' general arrogance and their attitude that healing is at best a gimmick or at worst dangerous which is so unhelpful.

There are good and bad in every profession. Unfortunately, most people on the NHS are assigned to the doctor in their area, so the quality of care they receive is a case of pot luck. This is not so with healers – people travel hundreds of miles to visit a good healer, something they would not do if they did not get the results they were seeking. I know, because when I was healing twelve hours a day, seven days a week, I still had a waiting list of three months or more. Miracles took place regularly, and still do through the distant healing service I offer throughout the world. I would have to employ a staff of twenty to keep records of the incredible results. As it is, I always burn the letters to ensure confidentiality.

I have been investigated by numerous people and have been interviewed incessantly. Would doctors be prepared to undergo this scrutiny, and to have the results printed in the national newspapers? I don't think so.

The majority of clashes between healers and the medical profession are caused by misunderstandings and by ignorance of the healing process. But there is another factor which the doctors fear – if they are seen to be sympathetic towards healers they would lose face, and perhaps be taken to task by the governing body of their profession.

In the past I have been asked to co-operate in medical experiments, particularly some to do with cells. However, when the results came through, showing that the structure of cells had been changed by the healing process, the project was dropped. What would have happened if the results had been negative? A damning piece in the *Lancet* perhaps?

I have met and worked with very talented scientists and physicians, and it has been a joy to converse with these very open-minded people, but even they confirmed that their lives could be made very difficult by their governing bodies if they went public with their beliefs.

Fear is our biggest enemy, and it has crippled many minds. Ordinary people who have been helped or cured through healing are petrified of telling their doctors the truth. This is so wrong, and it is why spiritual healing has never had the recognition it deserves. It is also why those with the gift are calling themselves everything but spiritual healers. It seems that as long as the healing process has an 'official' name it will be accepted, but I am afraid that no other name can be given to a process that goes back thousands of years. The miraculous cures of our forebears are readily accepted by religions around the world but are looked upon with disdain and suspicion if an ordinary man or woman happens to have the same gift today. I'm afraid that you cannot have it both ways.

I cannot repeat often enough that a whole healing depends on the healing of the spirit as well as the physical. There should be healing rooms in every doctor's surgery, and in every hospital. This would speed up a patient's recovery, and would save the NHS a tremendous amount of money. I believe that this *will* come at some stage, but I fear not soon enough.

Working conditions

Every day I am in communication with people throughout the world and I am appalled by the number who live in fear of losing their income. Unfortunately, nearly everyone at one time or another will have to face this problem. When things are really bad, lifestyles have to be changed, and in these instances one cannot worry about what family, friends or neighbours will think. Your life *can* be turned around, if you are willing to start again. Thousands have done it, and have survived. Those whose relationships have suffered the traumas of separation and divorce also have a chance to start again. Life is about change. Material possessions may give you pleasure, but they can also be an encumbrance you cannot afford.

I have personally had to start again many times in my life and have often felt that I would not survive the traumas. But I did. This has taught me that with hard work and determination you can not only survive but come out the other side with more compassion for others.

Do not become fearful under *any* circumstances. If you are prepared to give up a lifestyle that you can no longer maintain and look for opportunities anywhere in the world, then you will succeed. Fear imprisons the mind by dragging it down with too much inward thinking. This puts the brain under pressure and can result in loss of memory, as well as having a devastating effect on the nervous and immune systems. If you allow fear to take hold, then you will become incapacitated through illness. Do not let this happen to you.

There *is* an escape route, and that is through meditation or simple daydreaming. Outward thinking frees the mind, takes the pressure off the brain and body and every major organ, and rejuvenates each cell in the body. When the mind is free to travel in its own dimension, it usually returns with the answer to our problem. Sometimes an answer might seem unusual, but if it does then you know that it has come from a source other than yourself. Any new idea is worth investigating.

We are all guilty of blaming others for the predicaments that we find ourselves facing every day, but this is a great time-waster and life is too short. Put the past behind you and start again – and again, if necessary. The more changes you have, the younger and more confident you will feel.

There are many other areas of life in which people live in fear: women have lost their freedom to go out alone, fearful of the risk of attack from murderers and rapists; children have to be guarded from the very real danger of paedophiles; motorists have had the pleasure of a spin in the country ruined by the prospect of road rage; and workers in offices and factories are bullied by cruel bosses who abuse their positions of power. I deal with all these issues, and many more, in my book *A Mind of Your Own*, which shows how the power of the mind can be used to deal with over 200 common anxieties.

Summing up, we live in a violent society, and we need more powerful laws to stop the purging of young and old lives alike. To live in constant fear sears the soul and leads to terrible psychological damage. Laws need changing and quickly, because as they stand today they are desperately inadequate in stopping the scourge of fear that has everyone in its grip.

We must all fight for ourselves and for others, especially the unborn, or their lives will not be worth living.

14

THE MIND IS A FREE SPIRIT

FOR MANY YEARS I HAVE communicated with people who, for various reasons, have suffered brain damage and have been left in a comatose state. While some recover, some do not. Either way, I have been able to receive and pass on messages from the patient to family and friends, and even to the medical staff who have been looking after them. Even when the patient dies the messages continue, as they desperately try to keep open the lines of communication with their loved ones. Amazed at having survived death, they have an overwhelming need to prove it.

The patient is always the first to make contact. When the brain is incapacitated, the mind intermittently leaves the body. At this point it becomes a free spirit, and will automatically link into the mind of someone who can maintain close contact with family and friends.

I must emphasise that it is the patient who opens the channels every time, not the medium. I am always being asked to contact someone in spirit, but I cannot do this, and neither can any other medium. That is not how it works. No matter how frustrated the sitter may become at not receiving a message from a specific person, there is nothing the medium can do about it. We have to wait to be contacted. Then and only then can a medium pose questions that need an answer. Unlike this dimension where the mind is imprisoned within the physical body, the free mind has no boundaries and is therefore able to open up a line of communication whenever and wherever it is needed.

The physical body is a biological masterpiece which Mind Energy sustains until it begins to deteriorate. At the point of death the mind leaves, seeking other dimensions and in the case of reincarnation other bodies, enabling it to fulfil its destiny.

There is a very positive side to the comatose condition; whilst the mind is becoming accustomed to new surroundings, the patient does not suffer. When the mind leaves, or partially leaves the body, the electromagnetic charge from the mind to the brain weakens and the brain becomes unable to send messages via the nervous system. Feeling is shut off or is diminished. Also, scans have shown that the comatose body reacts favourably when healing has been given.

Many times whilst meditating, I have been contacted by someone in a coma who has given me not only their name but a diagnosis of their physical condition. When this happens I know that I will soon receive a letter from their family or friends asking for my help. Our world is a very small place in the Universe, and the messages I receive are from every corner of the globe.

Over the years I have received outstanding evidence from patients who have given a detailed description of the way in which their mind was able to view their own physical body, enter it, and give an accurate diagnosis whilst they were comatose. It is at this point, whilst they are experiencing this phenomenon, that they are introduced to 'mind to mind' contact and are able to contact someone like myself to whom they can pass on their thoughts and, if possible, their self-diagnosis. Their experiences were so profound that practically all of them told me that they had actually 'felt the hand of God'. Many were atheists before the coma, but with their recovery came a deep sense of the spiritual nature of the Universe and a peace hitherto unknown to them.

Some of the stories I have been told are quite hilarious, as many of the patients who recovered all their faculties were later able to recognise medical staff they had not known prior to their comatose state. This naturally left the doctors and nurses in a state of shock when snatches of conversations – some of a very personal nature – held at the patient's bedside were repeated back to them. Patients were also able to speak to the people who regularly cleaned their rooms as though they were old friends.

Once again this proves the ultimate freedom of spirit, of the soul, once it has left the physical body. Even those who do not survive the trauma are able to tell me that the injuries to their brain are incurable but, with their mind intact and an abiding sense of peace, they are happy to let go. Their only concern is for the living. They are aware at this point that if they can prove survival they will ease the pain of those they have left behind.

I remember being contacted by a little girl. She told me that she was six years old and that something was wrong with her heart. She did not give me her name, though she contacted me several times during the next two weeks, telling me about the beautiful birds and colours she had seen, and that she had made friends with another little girl. Two weeks later I received a letter from a mother in South Africa asking me to help her six-year-old daughter who had heart problems and who was in a coma. I told the mother that I would give her daughter healing. But I also knew that the child mentioned in the letter was the little girl I had been speaking to and that she would not survive – she had travelled too far into the other world. After her death I did not hear from her for four months, and then she came through, giving me survival evidence that I could pass on to her mother in South Africa. The evidence listed the names of her family and friends, and left the mother in no doubt that her daughter lived on. The peace, comfort and beauty that this kind of evidence brings really is 'out of this world'. Those who are left behind never forget, and I have been told that they are no longer afraid of dying or of the unknown; they know, as I do, that living and surviving on this planet is a lot harder than what we will find when we leave it.

Another interesting dimension to all this is the ability of the comatose patient who knows that they will not survive to communicate with me and give me detailed instructions for the kind of funeral they want. They tell me who they want to attend the service, the kind of flowers they would like, and of the need to help others by asking people to donate to a specific charity. I have also been asked to pass on messages to loved ones about their choice of clothes, especially the colours they would like their partners to wear.

Living in a dimension where colours are crystal clear and do not in any way mirror the kind of colours we see in *this* dimension, it is understandable that they should wish to influence those left behind. It has been made clear to me during survival evidence that they know that dark colours, especially brown and black, make it difficult to create a link, because dark colours have lower vibrations than bright colours. Black is nearly always worn at funerals, and the very people who want to feel their departed loved ones close at hand are unconsciously blocking them out.

Through survival evidence, the deceased have often described their funerals to me. Not only that, but they have been able to give the names of many friends and relatives who attended, and have made some very sarcastic remarks about those so-called friends who turned up. Some of these accounts were so entertaining that I could not contain my laughter when, true to type, the natural comedians could not resist giving impersonations of relatives and friends they had found infuriating. In death they still found a compulsive need to mimic them.

But to get back to when this chapter started, the most remarkable cases *are* those of people who manage to communicate whilst in a coma. I think you will find the following story illuminating.

Syd and Jean

Although my friends Syd and Jean lived in a neighbouring village to me, we rarely saw each other because of our busy lifestyles. So it was with some concern that I received a call one afternoon from Jean telling me that her husband had been taken seriously ill and was in a coma. I promised to visit him as soon as possible. My daughter Janet, who works with me, said that she would like to accompany me, so we downed tools for the day and drove to the hospital. There was an urgency about that journey which saddened me, because the diagnosis I was receiving was bad. I knew he was not going to survive.

Arriving at the hospital, we made our way to the Intensive Care Unit. When we entered the room we saw that Syd was attached to a life support machine. It did not look good at all.

Jean was in a state of shock, and we tried to comfort her. 'I can't believe this has happened,' she said. 'He was fine when he set out this morning.'

Although I was distressed to see Syd in this state, it was not unexpected. I had warned Jean six years previously that I could see disturbing energy patterns around her husband's head and tried to persuade her to encourage him to see the doctor and have his blood pressure checked. (I told Jean not to tell Syd about my diagnosis, because I can never see the sense of worrying someone unduly.) She persuaded him to have a medical check, it was found that he did have high blood pressure, and he was given medication.

Eighteen months later I saw them again, and the patterns were still there. I asked Jean whether he was still taking the tablets, because I was still worried about him. She assured me that he was.

Every time I thought about Syd after that, I knew that he would, at some time, have serious problems. Now my worst fears had been realised. He had suffered a brain haemorrhage and was in a coma.

I tried to comfort Jean and her step-daughter, but they were both in shock. Then Syd began to communicate with me. His mind was in great form and, though obviously amazed at finding himself in this distressing state, he was still able to air his views, which had always been quite varied. He reminded Jean of holidays they had taken together, reminiscing over the small things that make a partnership special. He told her not to try to sort out the mess in the garage, as he had been in the middle of putting the finishing touches to a conservatory that had just been built. 'Leave things as they are,' she was told. Whilst I was giving Jean the messages, my daughter Janet, who is also a medium, was also picking up messages from Syd, which she relayed to Jean as soon as I had finished. I could see at this point that although Jean was completely overwhelmed, she was also elated. She understood exactly what was happening as both she and Syd had received survival evidence, clairvoyance and healing from me over the years. But even though this occasion was very sad and traumatic, we were later able to laugh at the turn of events. I am sure that Syd was sharing in the laughter as we recounted the many times that he avoided the subject of my healing and mediumship, apparently ignoring the fact that I had been able to give him exceptional evidence of the survival of his father. He did not understand it, and I think he was frightened of it – when death is mentioned it is amazing how many people want to pretend it will never happen to them, even though it is an inevitable event for all of us. Yet here he was communicating through *me*, the last person he would have wished to engage in this kind of conversation when he was alive.

It is interesting to note that neither Janet nor I had any previous knowledge of the varied messages that were given to us. Janet had no contact with Jean, and I had not seen her for two years, but every single word was accepted by Jean as being absolutely authentic.

After this evidence, it became obvious that Syd was not going to survive and the life support machine was turned off.

Jean has had remarkable evidence from Syd since his death, all over the phone from me as we are both extremely busy people. From the beginning he encouraged her to take up her watercolour painting again and said that he would always be with her to give encouragement and inspiration. Recently, during one of our conversations, he told her how much he liked her latest picture, proving once again that he is still taking care of her. Jean has told me that the painting is the best she has ever done.

Jean's story

One November morning, as my husband was leaving the house, I said, 'Goodbye, enjoy your day.' He had recently retired, and was helping a conservation group renovate an old windmill.

'You too,' he replied, smiling. I did not know that these would be the last words I would ever hear from him.

I tidied the house and then drove to my daughter's home as we were going to have a day out in Brighton. When we returned in the afternoon, I received a telephone message that my husband, Syd, had become ill and had been taken to hospital. I was told not to worry, that it was 'just for tests'. My daughter and I immediately hurried to collect a few things from my own home before going to the hospital.

I found on arrival that Syd had been taken to the Neurology Department. To my great distress I found that he had suffered a severe brain haemorrhage and was seriously ill. I saw him just before he lost all consciousness.

I was told by the staff to go home and collect the

medication that he had been taking, which I did. However, on my return I was taken aside by a nurse and doctor and told that he had suffered another haemorrhage and that he was going to die. Suffering from extreme shock, all I could do was stroke his head. He was now in the Intensive Care Unit, linked up to life support machines. There was so much I wanted to say to him, and I longed to hear his voice again.

Later, I rang my family and friends, including my dear friend Betty Shine. As always, she was wonderful and supportive, and told me that she would do everything possible to help Syd. Just after this conversation, and to the amazement of the staff, he did improve, although I was told that even if he did recover he was so brain-damaged that he would never be able to walk or talk. I could not think of a worse scenario for Syd, as he was a great talker and storyteller.

It was at this point that Betty and her daughter Janet arrived at the hospital. As soon as Betty saw him, she said, 'He's gone, Jean.' She knew his mind had left, even though the machines were keeping his heart pumping. Janet said, 'There is so much power coming from him.' Syd then communicated with me through Betty and her daughter for an hour. He mentioned holidays and situations that had been very important to us both and where we had been very happy. He wanted me to remember the good times. At no time did he ever mention anything that Betty and Janet could possibly have known. That was the most remarkable thing about the whole situation. It was most definitely Syd – at his best. I knew then that he would never die, that his mind lived on.

The amusing thing is that Syd had had very little time for 'life after death' theories. He pooh-poohed it all, even though he had received remarkable survival evidence from Betty. Thankfully, she always laughed at his scepticism.

A few days after his death, Betty rang me and said that Syd wanted to talk with me. The first thing he said was, 'I never thought I'd end up here' – typical Syd humour. He gave me a commentary of how he had felt whilst they were rushing him to hospital, about the pain in his head. He spoke of a cabinet he was making, which was in itself incredible survival evidence, as Betty had not seen us for two years. He wanted his grandson to have a cricket bat to remember him by, and mentioned the bright red colour of his hair. There were special, very private messages for myself. Betty could not possibly have known any of these facts.

To know, without doubt, that the mind is still intact after the death of the physical body is the greatest comfort for anyone who has lost a loved one. I have had this confirmed by a great teacher – Betty Shine. I have found that every conversation with Betty is a whole education, and a great privilege.

The ability to make a correct diagnosis is solely due to my ability as a clairvoyant. And it is my clairvoyance that enables me to see clearly when the mind has finally left the physical body. Many people are left on life support machines even though their minds have gone to a better place.

Talented mediums can be invaluable to a family when someone is in a coma. If they had been accepted into the medical profession long ago, their exceptional gifts could have prevented much suffering. One can only hope that if someone in the family has a friend who is a medium, that they will turn to them whenever they need spiritual support.

15

THE HEALING POWER OF LIGHT

And the earth was without form, and void,
And God said, Let there be light.

I HAVE ALREADY TOUCHED upon the subject of light in this book, especially the pure white light that surrounds the head of the patient after treatment. In my previous books I have given detailed descriptions of the light that appeared in my healing room, and explained the incredible results I have obtained using my 'laser beam' method of dealing with every kind of physical problem in both direct and distant healing. And thousands of my patients have spoken about the brilliance of the light in my eyes whilst healing and giving survival evidence. They see and feel a power that they cannot understand.

In fact, it is this brilliance and power that has enabled me to form the 'laser beam' that has cured so many people over the years. So what is the source of this brilliant light and power? The answer is that it is a 'mind-to-mind' contact between the spiritual realm and my own personality, a contact which forms a unique partnership. The same power enables me to shape my own 'mind tools' detailed in Chapter 10, 'A Whole Bag of Tools'. (Interestingly, hospitals now also successfully use their own type of laser treatment for various ailments.)

I have treated more patients than I can remember who have suffered terrible depression in the dark winter months because of the lack of light. Yet whenever they had healing, their depression would lift and the benefits would last several weeks or more. At that time I did not understand the problem and neither did the medical profession. Now it is universally recognised as SAD (Seasonal Affective Disorder) and is known to be caused by lack of light.

Throughout my long career as a professional healer, I have also taught and written about the incredible cures that have taken place when a patient has been enveloped by coloured cosmic rays – colours, incidentally, not chosen by myself or the patient. It has been possible to feel the different vibrations that accompanied the colours that were being used for a whole spectrum of illnesses. My healing room would often be flooded with bright sunflower-coloured energies that simulated waves. Patients often remarked that they felt as though they were being washed back and forth by a tide, an experience similar to bathing in the sea.

Through the ages, proof of the healing power of light and colour healing has been set before the scientific and medical establishments by healers, past and present. The evidence was ignored. But we were right, and it is obvious now that someone has listened, learned and experimented with our findings. But in many ways they are still light years away from the experiences of professional healers. Medical practitioners are finally following in the footsteps of healers, who have been using colour healing for centuries. The doctors who follow their own individual paths to their enlightenment, think up the most extraordinary devices to play the light through coloured paper and plastic. They are apparently getting good results when they apply the colour therapy to physical ailments, although I must remind them that healers have used their own form of colour therapy for decades with excellent results. The practice is not a new one, but all credit to them for getting there in the end!

The coloured rays that permeated my healing room from the beginning of my healing career were so unexpected – and so beautiful – that I felt privileged to have that added bonus every day. It was quite some time before I decided to experiment with colour therapy on my patients, but when I did the results were extremely encouraging. I had determined that one patient required the colour green to quiet her nervous system, so I conjured up the colour with my mind and proceeded to flood her body with the energies. At first green did appear, but then it was quickly overshadowed by red. I was astonished, because red would have been the last colour I would have thought this particular patient needed. However, through mediumistic diagnosis, I was told that the patient had cancer and that red was the appropriate colour for this disease. At this time the patient did not know she had cancer, but when I encouraged her to see a specialist the diagnosis was confirmed. Even though I did not agree with her decision to refuse medical treatment and, at her request, carried on with the colour therapy, she did make a full recovery. I do not believe that it was purely the colour healing that gave such a good result. One has also to take into consideration the incredible light that is always present when healing is being given. Now I understand that red light-dependent, photodynamic therapy, combined with light-sensitising drugs, is the latest in cancer therapy. One of the positive sides of this treatment is that it destroys only the malignant cells, and can safely be repeated if necessary.

Although it is fascinating to read about how much energy, time and money have been spent experimenting with light therapy, and thrilling to read of the success rate when treating the sick, it is also frustrating to know that the success stories that healers have written about for many years – through a similar but more natural light therapy – have been ignored by scientists and medics alike. Even now, I do not believe they really understand what is happening.

Whilst giving hands-on healing, the coloured cosmic rays come through of their own accord, obviously triggered by the mind link to the cosmos – in other words – the Universal Mind. This is a more reliable method of healing through colour by far than the hit-and-run method used by scientists.

Through my experience with colour I was able to experiment with coloured scarves and fabric. I asked my patients to buy a scarf or find a piece of material that they could carry around with them all the time. The colour was dependent on the diagnosis. When they returned for their next appointment I was intrigued by their experiences: some people saw coloured rays being played upon them in their own homes; sometimes a variation of the recommended colour was seen; others saw a completely different colour to the one I had suggested. I realised then that the colour they had been using was simply a key to open the door to the cosmic rays, and a force far greater than my own was giving the correct colour necessary for their condition. I was happy for them to change the colour, if they wished, as I realised that I was still the pupil. I learnt a lot from this experiment.

When colour is being used in healing, it does attract like to like. One only has a look at the natural colours in our environment – brightly coloured flowers, the many variations of green foliage, orange sunsets, blue skies, varying qualities of light – the list is endless. These colours do not just happen. They are part and parcel of the cosmic rays of light that enable the genetic make-up of plants to blossom and to colour our lives. The difference in the structure of plants is the deciding factor in what cosmic colour it attracts. If a plant is kept in the dark, the flower buds will remain white and will not open. It needs light to flourish and produce coloured flowers.

Through meditation I have seen true colours, untainted by the dense atmosphere that we have here in this dimension, and have learnt that we have lost because of the pollution of our planet.

I have often written about the incredible blue energy that not only pervades the healing room but is also absorbed by the patient.

In my own healing room it became so dense at times that I was completely screened and could not be seen by others in the room until I had finished healing. Now, every intensive care unit is bathed in a blue light, because of the calming effect it has on the patients, although those in the medical profession admit that they do not understand why it works. Perhaps they should listen to healers, who could certainly enlighten them!

I believe that scientists and medical practitioners still have a long way to go before they can advance their colour healing theories. They ought to realise that it is not the light shining through the piece of coloured paper that achieves results but the interaction of thought processes, combined with cosmic rays. For example, if one thinks of a colour, this is mind-set, and the mind links in with the cosmos – from which all life, light and colour originate – to attract the same colour energies. The piece of coloured paper is really only a focus for their thoughts – but what would their peers say if they told them they were only 'thinking colour' to achieve results? They would also have to accept that there is an energy that processes all our thoughts and actions and contains data from not only this life but past lives too – the 'infinite mind'.

Unfortunately for them, to advance along these lines of investigation one has to accept a spiritual element. One can only hope that the scientific and spiritual principles will one day come together as one for their advancement. We are desperately in need of a more enlightened world. It is time for everyone to share their knowledge and to listen to each other. It would certainly create a more caring environment for the future of mankind, and bring even more light into our lives.

16

THE SALLY FRANKENBERG STORY

IT WAS A VERY STRANGE DAY. I had been asked to give a talk at the Royal Air Force Club in Piccadilly for the International Club of Air Force Wives, a charitable organisation.

After much thought I accepted, but not before I had spoken at great length with the Chairman, discussing whether or not they would be the right kind of audience for the subject matter of my lecture, part of which would be about mediumship. She assured me that nearly all the people in the audience would have lost someone, and that I would be warmly received.

I had never had any contact with the RAF, but as a teenager working in London during the last stages of the Second World War, I had been asked to help out at the Polish Air Force Club, writing letters, reading newspapers and chatting to these very lonely men, many of whom had lost all the members of their families. So I felt confident that there would be an affinity between the audience and myself. However, while travelling to London for this event, I experienced feelings that usually depicted some kind of disaster. At one point I wanted to turn back, but felt that I could not let people down in this way.

When I arrived it became immediately apparent that something was amiss, and that my intuitive feelings had, as usual, been correct. Apparently, the Chairman who had engaged me had left, and the present Chairman had not been made aware of my booking. I offered to leave but was assured that I was still welcome – even though my intuition was telling me that this was not so.

During lunch I was introduced to the other guest speakers, whom I will not name here because of their status, but they obviously had no interest in me. Things were going very badly indeed.

The first two guest speakers gave their speeches, and then the microphone was handed to me. I began by introducing myself – when there was an almighty bang overhead, as though the ceiling was about to fall in. It shuddered so much that everyone in the room became alarmed. I switched off the mike and the noise stopped. I knew then that my spirit team were not happy with the way I had been treated. This sort of thing had happened before, in similar circumstances. I tried to explain this to the audience, but the secretary insisted it was the microphone. I had to laugh. How on earth could a microphone make the ceiling of a very substantial and solid building shake, rattle and roll? For that is precisely what happened. She handed me another microphone, but when I tried to speak again the racket was ten times worse. The Chairman called the porter, and asked him to go upstairs and have a look around. He came down and told us that there was no one upstairs at all, that the rooms above were empty. Eventually I had to speak without the microphone, which was very difficult. At the end the audience clapped, probably with relief, but we had all been made aware that my spirit team were very angry at the kind of treatment that had been meted out to me. All I wanted to do was leave.

Much to my amazement, however, this was not to be, because a huge queue had formed of people who wanted to speak to me. Before I knew it, the first person was shaking my hand. I thought at first glance that it was Jane Seymour, the actress, and I wondered why she was attending this lunch. When the young woman introduced herself, I remarked on her amazing likeness to the actress.

She laughed, and said, 'I'm Jane's sister, Annie,' and, taking the hand of an older woman, she introduced me to her mother, Mieke. They told me that they loved my books and that they would like to meet me again sometime. We had very little time together as there were others waiting to speak to me, but they were very kind and assured me that my talk had been successful. But as they turned away, something made me touch Mieke on the shoulder and give her my telephone number. I said, 'I think you will need this.' Little did we know how soon that would be.

Annie and Mieke's story

Annie: My mother is a member of the International Club of Air Force Wives, and when she told me that Betty Shine was going to give a talk at the Club in Piccadilly, I was delighted and could not wait to hear her speak, as I have had a lifelong interest in health and healing.

However, it was obvious from the outset that the audience were not aware of who Betty was, and I was ashamed of the way she was being treated by her hosts, who virtually ignored her.

When the other well-known guest speakers had finished their speeches, it was time for Betty to speak.

Mieke: When Betty began to speak, loud sounds emanated from the ceiling of this very solid building. I can only describe it as sounding like hammers banging on metal pipes. The noise was horrendous, and we could not hear her at all.

The Chairman left her seat and, taking the microphone out of Betty's hand, tested it by speaking into it. It was perfect, so Betty tried again, only to be silenced once more by the same terrible noise. It was banging and thumping so much that the ceiling shook. The charade continued, with the microphone being handed to the Chairman, who found it to be normal, and back to Betty and the deafening noises.

Eventually someone was despatched to the front desk, to ask whoever it was thumping on the ceiling of our room to stop. They were told that there were no workmen on the premises. Then the porter was asked to go upstairs and search the premises, which he did, only to find that the upper rooms were deserted.

In the meantime, another microphone was tried and tested before being handed to Betty, with the words, 'This one is foolproof.' Famous last words. Unfortunately, the noises would not abate. Betty told me later that she could hardly contain her mirth, as this kind of phenomenon always occurred when her spirit team felt that she had been slighted. They were telling her that she should leave.

Fortunately for us Betty stayed, and gave her talk without the microphone, which was difficult for her because it was a very large room.

When she had finished her lecture, Annie and I were at the front of the long queue that had formed to speak to her. Her first words to Annie were, 'I thought you were Jane Seymour, the actress. You look like twins.' Annie explained that Jane was her sister. Then she introduced me to Betty. We shook hands, and I asked her whether she could give me private healing sessions, but she explained that writing her books and dealing with correspondence from around the world meant that she had been forced to give up contact healing in favour of distant healing, from which she said she had excellent results. I accepted the offer of distant healing, and agreed to tune in to her healing network.

Annie: I had recently begun a four year course in homoeopathy, so I asked Betty if this was the correct direction for me. I felt that she would tell me the truth, as I believed in her humanity and integrity. I also asked her if I could be a healer. She replied by saying, 'You can heal your family and friends now – just do it.' Then she repeated it.

Mieke: Annie and I thanked Betty for her time and then walked away, as there were many other people who wished to speak with her. Suddenly Betty came after me, put her hands on my shoulders and kissed me. She then scribbled her telephone number on a piece of paper and said, 'I think you might need this.'

That same night, my other daughter, Sally, was taken ill whilst attending a concert with a girlfriend in Reading. Apparently, just before the interval she had felt alternately very hot and cold and had developed an excruciating headache. She had collapsed after putting her head between her knees. An ambulance was called, and she was taken to the nearest hospital in Reading.

Annie: The same night as Betty's lecture, I had gone to bed only to be woken by the phone. My sister Sally's girlfriend was on the other end, telling me that Sally was in hospital; she was rambling, not able to speak properly. I felt my jaw turn to stone, and made her repeat the address of the hospital six times. I just could not take it in.

My husband and I dressed and drove to Reading. When we arrived, we found Sally still lying on a trolley in Emergency, not making any sense. From that moment I stayed with her and made sure that she received prompt attention. I held her hand, explaining every procedure that she had to endure, until they took her away for a scan. When the medical staff returned I was told that Sally had suffered a brain haemorrhage and that the chances of her recovery were slim. She probably would not survive the night.

After they had wheeled my sister into a ward of desperately ill people and pulled the curtains around her bed, I remembered Betty's words of just twelve hours ago, 'You can heal your family and friends now – just do it.' I suddenly felt elated. Instead of being utterly helpless, there was something that I could do. I stood up, cupped my hands in the air above Sally's head where the internal bleeding was taking place, and willed her to get better, for the blood to be reabsorbed and for the rupture to mend. I did this all night.

I waited until first light to phone my mother and tell her the news. I believe that bad news is never quite so bad if there is some light. I had already called my sister Jane in America, and she and her husband were on their way on the first plane out.

In the morning the doctors reassessed Sally and decided that her condition was good enough for her to be transferred to the brilliant Radcliffe Infirmary in Oxford, where some of the best brain surgeons in the country perform their miracles every day. On arrival she had an MRI scan on her brain which showed that she had two aneurysms. The surgeon explained to us that he would clip the second aneurysm when he operated on the one that had ruptured. However, the operation itself could not take place for several days, because they would be unable to locate the exact spot until some of the blood had been reabsorbed. Also, the veins had gone into spasm, so they had put Sally on a drip to encourage maximum oxygenation of the blood that was not able to circulate through the brain. The situation was still dangerous. At any time the haemorrhage could recur and kill her.

Mieke: After I had visited Sally, I went home to fetch Betty Shine's telephone number. When she answered, I explained that I had spoken to her the day before. Betty laughed and said, 'Of course I know who you are.' She then told me that she had expected something to happen, as she had been urged to give me her telephone number. She never normally gave this out as it was ex-directory. When I had finished telling her about the terrible trauma Sally was experiencing, she told me not to worry about the second aneurysm, as she would 'take care of it'.

When I had finished speaking with Mieke I replaced the receiver and did what I always do when I am asked to help people who are in a coma: I sat down and went into a deep meditative state. This way it would be easy to bypass the injuries to the brain and link in with the mind, which would, through shock, have joined the elaborate and little-understood Universal communication system.

Linking in with Sally, I was pleased to find that she was at peace. I then went through the process of diagnosing the energy system so that I could slip her into the healing network that I had set up many years ago. This bypasses the physical and can bring about a whole healing instead of purely physical healing.

When I had finished, I saw a young man sitting at the side of her bed. He told me that he had been a friend of Sally's, was the son of Mieke's friends and had died young. This was verified later. He told me that he was anxious to help Sally and would be by her side until she was well.

This contact was invaluable to me, as he would be able to communicate with me at any time if he felt that my intervention could prevent further deterioration, which is exactly what happened over the ensuing months.

Jane Seymour came over from America to be with her sister, and we talked over the telephone. She thanked me for everything I was doing for Sally, but it was obvious that she was very distressed, as were all the family. They were by Sally's side constantly. I know that in this case nobody could have done more for her than her family and friends and, of course, the medical team who were trying to save her life.

Time and again the operation to remove the blood clots had to be cancelled because of her precarious condition. During this period I was communicating with Sally and was able to tell her family how she felt and how things were going in general. I was also able to reassure them that she was going to recover and that her brain would not be affected in any way, always a worry in these cases.

Mieke: Finally, the doctors were able to operate on Sally. When it was over I asked the surgeon if he had clipped the second aneurysm, as he had said that he would. He told me that the aneurysm was not there any more and that he was very surprised by this – the MRI scan had definitely shown it to be there.

The next time I contacted Betty, I had to tell her that Sally's condition had worsened, that she was now paralysed and could not speak. She simply said, 'I will see what I can do.' I thanked her. Against the odds, Sally recovered from the paralysis and got her speech back. She is now completely normal again, and everyone involved in Sally's healing thinks that it is a miracle.

There is no doubt that the love that flowed from Betty's healing, through Sally's sisters and my own hands stimulated the natural healing functions of the body and spirit. Whilst we held her, I felt a tingling sensation in my hands, and Annie felt the same sensation around her hairline and up her arms. And we remembered Betty's words: 'You can heal your family and friends now – just do it.'

There was another interesting development. After the operation, Annie asked the surgeon whether it would be all right for her to give Sally homoeopathic Arnica for the bruising. We could see from the other patients in the ward who had undergone brain surgery that the resulting bruising and swelling was horrific, and the nurse had told us that Sally would look like the Elephant Man. So Annie gave her regular doses of Arnica 30cc every two hours. The swelling never happened. Every day the doctors would come in to see her at 7.00 a.m., and they were constantly surprised when they saw that there was no bruising or swelling.

My whole family is extremely grateful to Betty Shine for her love and support during that awful time, and especially for the encouragement she gave us when we needed it most.

There is so much more to this story than I could put into this book. One thing I cannot impress on people enough is that when someone is in a coma they remain aware of everything that is being said and done for them. They are also aware of the people around them and of their emotions. It is most important that everyone – family, friends, relatives, the medical profession and any-one else near the patient – should be extremely positive. Several ex-coma patients have told me that they were acutely aware that their relatives did not expect them to live. In their out-of-body state they were not particularly worried, but they were saddened by it because though they knew they were being cared for by loved ones that had died, they could not reassure those who sat anxiously by their bedside hour after hour in a state of despair. Many have told me that they learnt of the possible death of their physical body by listening to hospital cleaners as they worked in the room.

For those who are in despair for a loved one who has suffered as Sally did, or for those who might do so in the future, I hope her story will give you the faith and strength to carry on and to try contact healing for yourself. Above all, never give up hope, and never stop trying to alleviate the pain and suffering felt by everyone in these circumstances. There are so many stories about coma victims recovering when their relatives had been told that there was no hope. Miracles do still happen, and they could happen to you and your loved ones.

17

OUT-OF-BODY EXPERIENCES

AFTER AN ACCIDENT IT IS sometimes possible that the victim's mind will detach itself from the physical body. This occurs more often than one would suppose, and the incredible stories are so varied that it is obvious that the experience has been unique to the victim and not one that can be compared to that of anyone else.

It is a similar situation to that of being in a deep meditative state. The victims look down on the scene as an observer, not as the owner of the injured body. It is only later, when they are unable to communicate with other people at the scene, that they feel uncomfortable and angry, believing that everyone is either deaf or deliberately ignoring them. In this state the mind is still in close proximity to the body, but it is rather like having a thin sheet of cling film between the two dimensions. This is the first stage between life and death.

Mike was a young man in his early twenties. He was addicted to speeding in his car and this addiction caused a terrible crash which left him in a near-death state. He wandered around the scene of the accident with apparent ease, but was angry because the medics and firemen at the scene ignored his cynical remarks about their 'trying to raise the dead' when he was obviously okay. He asked them to look at him dancing around. 'Do I look dead to you?' he asked them. He told me that he was engulfed by frustration when he realised that no one could hear him. He also told me of his fear when, in desperation, he touched one of the medics and his hand went right through the other man's body, as though it simply did not exist. All around him was space and people hurrying back and forth, and although he was standing in the middle of the carnage he was ignored. For them he simply was not there. Even when they lifted his body from the ground and carried it towards the waiting ambulance, he tried to follow. When he thought he was firmly ensconced in the ambulance, he found that it had somehow left without him. He was still standing on the road. He tried to tell those who were picking up the pieces of tangled wreckage that the medics had stolen his body and left him behind, but of course they could not hear him. Then he lost all sense of time. When he regained his senses he was standing at the side of a bed, looking down at himself. His body was surrounded by medical staff rushing around, attaching machines and tubes. He felt tired of trying to communicate, and went to sleep.

Suddenly he was flying toward a deep blue sky. He flew higher and higher until he felt someone place a smooth silky wrap around his body. It was warm, and he had the feeling that he had somehow gone back to the womb.

When he finally returned to his physical body, his mother told him that he had been in a coma for five days.

Although fifteen years have passed since his accident, Mike told me that it is still as clear to him today as it had been then. But, most important of all, he would never again fear death, and without that fear his life had become more carefree and relaxed.

Diana also had an Out-of-Body Experience when she was electro-cuted from a fault in her iron. She told me that one minute she was standing ironing, the next she was floating around the ceiling of her home, looking down at her dog who had gone completely berserk. She tried to comfort him, but could not get down on to the floor. According to her calculations she had been floating for about ten minutes before she woke up, lying on the floor and feeling as though she had been hit over the head with a hammer. The dog had disappeared and was found skulking beneath the dining room table, also apparently suffering from shock.

Animals can in fact see spirit entities, so it had been a double shock for him to suddenly see his mistress attached to the ceiling. He must have felt that his world had turned completely upside down!

Chris was out walking in the countryside with his dogs when the weather suddenly changed and he found himself battling against an extremely strong wind. He said that it felt like a mini tornado. The next thing he remembers is being inside his house and trying to speak to his wife and children. He was furious because they completely ignored him. He distinctly remembers his wife preparing the evening meal and watching the children doing their homework.

Then he heard a gruff voice say, 'Thank goodness you've come round. I found you lying here with a huge branch beside you, obviously brought down by this awful storm. Where do you live? I will take you home.'

When he arrived home, supported by the gentleman who had found him, his wife grumbled because he was late for his meal. His rescuer said, 'He's had a nasty accident, lady. He needs to sit down and rest.'

Chris told his wife that he had seen her preparing the meal and had seen the children studying. She replied that the bang had obviously affected his brain – until he described in detail what had been going on in their house whilst he had been away. She eventually believed him.

Over the years I have heard hundreds of similar stories and, of course, can totally relate to them because of my own OBEs through meditation, healing and mediumship. I find it hard to understand, when so many thousands of such stories have been recorded, that there is still such scepticism about the truth. I ask myself time and time again, 'When will they ever learn?'

18

SPIRIT ENTITIES

ALTHOUGH THERE ARE many sceptics around, I have never yet met anyone who is not totally fascinated by stories of visitations by spirit entities – though they may not wish them to appear to them in person! I can understand that. But I don't understand why they should be so afraid of family and friends who loved them so much that they just want to say, 'Don't cry for me. Look! I'm here.' What possible harm could come from their loved ones? They have not suddenly changed into the devil – they're still the same people they were before they died. We actually have more to fear from people who are still alive than we do from spirits.

Because of the ridiculous stories that appear in newspapers and horror films, perhaps it is the fear of possession that worries people? I hope it will allay those fears if I tell you that I do not believe possession can take place unless someone is already undergoing severe mental trauma or is an alcoholic or drug addict, because we only attract energies that are like-to-like. As the mind is energy, one would therefore be attracting a like-mind. If there is a presence that you find disturbing, you should analyse your own thoughts in an honest and down-to-earth way. If you are sincere in your wish to create a happy atmosphere and environment around you, then you may have to change your lifestyle, but if this change gives you the peace that you need, then the effort will have been worthwhile. Do not blame the bad spirits, because you invited them in with your own negativity. Healing can certainly help cast away unwanted influences, but it is up to the individual concerned to find a permanent solution.

There are mischievous spirits, usually children, who are often invited in through the mind of a child. You should never under-estimate the power of a child's mind, nor of the power of the mind in general. If you mess around with the mind, you will be playing with fire. I know, because I have studied Mind Energy for so many years now that it has taken over a huge chunk of my life. It continues to fascinate me to this day, and I am still learning. Never abuse this powerful force for it could ultimately destroy you.

Through the years I have listened to amazing accounts of the many ways in which people have practised mind control. On further investigation it has turned out that they were doing it for purely selfish reasons, to control the thoughts and actions of those around them. If you wish to discipline the mind to enhance your ability to control your *own* life, that is a different matter, but on no account should you try to control anyone else. If you make someone a prisoner of your mind, then you will become their gaoler. You will find that this is a full-time occupation, one that can only end in disaster.

Exactly the same thing occurs with spirit entities. If you acknowledge any negative spirits around you, you are giving them the support they need to control you, to take over your mind. If this is happening to you, then take the control back into your own hands. You should ignore them, and tell them mentally that they are not welcome, and blot them out by visualising their arrest by two positive spirits. Watch as they are taken away and removed from your space. By ignoring negative situations, whether they are in this dimension or another, you will diminish the hold such people may have over you.

It is much the same when people argue, and the same accusations are repeated again and again, like a merry-go-round. The argument will not stop until someone refuses to accept the negativity which has caused such havoc, bad feelings, and vindictive behaviour. It has to be stopped at some point, the sooner the better. So just walk away from it.

Messages from spiritual realms can also be difficult to handle. I have had thousands of messages from spiritual sources giving advice which — although encouraging in concept — may be extremely difficult to follow on a daily basis, especially when the message concerns more than one person. But I do remember messages, and act on them at a later date if at all possible, providing I believe that the actions I take will not embarrass others.

One must always remember that we inhabit an extremely difficult and dangerous planet, and that the dark forces are not spirits but human beings who should know better. These are the people one should fear, the people who will eventually destroy this planet, not those in the spiritual realm.

Throughout my years as a medium and healer, I have been asked to describe spirit entities. When one is communicating with a client then this is easy — I can give the client a detailed description of the communicator, which they can accept. But it is difficult to describe all the types of entities I have seen, because they are all so different. I have seen spirit entities who appear to be solid human beings; I have seen entities who are transparent but who still have a human form; others are seemingly fluid energy beings whose shape changes all the time, as though they are trying to hold the thought to be able to project an image but aren't quite succeeding. For loved ones to accept that a spirit entity is someone they have known, a clear mental picture of that person is necessary for the medium to be able to give a good description. However, if the entity cannot hold the thought — for it is only by projecting an image of themselves as they used to be that a picture can be built up — they cannot show themselves. It depends entirely on the strength of mind of the communication. Being in a different dimension does not change the strength of their mind, it will be exactly the same as it was when they died. Only through progression can the mind change. This does not in any way hamper the evidence, because the identity of the communicator will already have been established.

Spirit communicators sometimes give a clear picture of themselves, only for the sitter to reject them; but inevitably they are accepted later by a family member or friend. If someone needs to communicate, they will use anyone they can to get their message through to the people they want to speak to.

In this respect, some of the survival evidence that I have given has been hilarious, with every word being rejected out of hand and the recipient repeatedly saying, 'I do not know this person.' But in nearly every case someone has eventually recognised the communicator. I remember one lady who insisted that she did not know or recognise the person giving the messages. But when she repeated the entire incident to a friend, all was revealed – it had been her friend's father. When this friend subsequently came for a sitting, her father came through loud and clear, and gave her the most incredible evidence that lasted for over two hours. The first lady laughingly remarked that her friend had received the kind of evidence she herself would have died for, yet she had nothing. Happily, someone special did come through for her at a later date.

I believe that sightings and survival evidence from spirit entities are the most powerful evidence for the existence of the infinite mind. These people have died and are no longer part of this particular dimension. Their bodies, including the brain, have disintegrated and are no more, and yet with the power of thought they can project a remembered image of themselves, passing on evidence that proves beyond a shadow of a doubt that they still exist.

For hundreds of years mediums have been passing on such messages to friends and relatives, messages that contain private data that could not possibly have come from anyone but the deceased. But instead of being nurtured because of this incredible talent, the mediums have been used and abused by people who through their ignorance have condemned them out of hand. That is why I write books – to educate those who know little or nothing about the paranormal. I believe that individuals should find out all they can about any subject before they begin to criticise other people's beliefs. Otherwise, what can they base their criticism on?

One of the biggest problems today is that a huge number of people do not read and they have forgotten how to listen. They make assumptions without facts, and when the facts are explained they simply stop listening, because their ego tells them it must be incorrect. No matter what evidential material against their ideas is proffered, it is instantly rejected.

Many friends have told me that whenever the subject of healing and mediumship has been introduced at a dinner party, someone (usually male) is rude and dismissive. One friend said, with a certain amount of humour, 'You'd have thought I was talking about mass murder!' What on earth do these people *think* we do? The mind boggles.

There is also another side of the coin – where those who have been in the company of a medium for a short while declare that they too have been given the gift of clairvoyant sight and can see and hear spirits. There is not much one can say to that, except to appear to accept their delusions and hope that, one day, it *will* happen for them. But there is a danger here, because if they continue to delude themselves, others will become involved and it will be difficult for them to extricate themselves when they find that people will eventually ask for real evidence. Many talented mediums do not have clairvoyant sight and cannot actually see those who are giving survival evidence. They can only give a sensitive description of the kind of personality that is communicating with them. This does not make them any less of a medium than one who can see, but it does illustrate how this gift cannot just occur spontaneously. For those with clairvoyant sight there will always have been a history of peculiar happenings from childhood. The talent is mainly hereditary, and has been shaped and strengthened by use throughout the ages.

This is why the information available from such people should have been taken seriously over the years and not ridiculed. If this had been the case I would not be writing this book. The whole world would be enlightened and know that the mind is a free energy that can leave the body when we sleep to rejuvenate both itself and our bodies when it returns; it would know that, by thought, we can project ourselves into the Universe and have an Out-of-Body Experience; it would know that we can use a single thought via a Universal network to give healing anywhere on this planet; finally, the world would know that when the brain dies, this energy continues to survive, that it cannot die.

I have often been asked how so many dead people manage to find room in the Universe. It is because the mind is energy, and when it is in its own energy dimension it can, by a single thought, reduce its size to that of a pinhead or expand into infinity. These minds do not inhabit one dimension or one Universe – there are hundreds of dimensions and other Universes. That is how my spirit mentors have explained it to me. Although these explanations may seem simplistic, I do not think that I or anyone else on this planet would be able to understand everything that we could be told about the spirit dimensions, even if we received all the information we would like, so we have to make do with the little that we can absorb. It still does not alter the fact that studies of Mind Energy must continue.

For me, the research will never stop. This is not an unselfish path on my part, because I find the subject fascinating and I am still being given answers to questions I asked years ago. Most important of all, I like to think that by passing on the lessons I have learnt, it will help others to find their own path of enlightenment.

19

HYPNOSIS

IT IS IMPOSSIBLE TO understand hypnosis without understanding the nature of the mind. Psychologists, neuropsychologists, imaging experts who use PET scanning (Positron Emission Tomography) and many scientific establishments have all come up with theories about hypnosis that are fascinating, but which are all missing the point. Unable to see or study Mind Energy, they rely on machines which can only measure brain activity and blood flow, and on an array of 'thought forms' from the control's mind to that of his subject.

Some hypnotists use their eyes as a means of control, stage hypnotists use their eyes and the bright lights of the theatre, while others hold a bright object in front of the subject and ask them to concentrate on it.

It is said that the eyes are the mirror of the soul. Because I believe that the mind and soul are one, I agree with this hypothesis. This is not blind belief on my part. I have been told by many thousands of my clients that whilst healing and giving survival evidence, the colour and brightness of my eyes changes all the time as the different personalities who are healing or communicating through me link their minds with mine and we become as one. I know in an instant when an evil mind, dead or alive, links in with mine, and my instinctive reaction – both mentally and physically – is to reject that person totally.

This is why the study of the hypnotic state concerns me, because scientists, the medical profession and stage hypnotists cannot possibly know what kind of person they are dealing with unless they are aware of the vibrations. It is argued by the medical establishment that hypnosis should only be given by qualified doctors, but the only way to give hypnosis safely is to learn, intuitively, how to feel the vibrations of the subject. This cannot be done with machines.

Studies of healers have shown that the patient takes on the same calming vibrational rate as that of the healer. One can only therefore imagine what happens to those people who take part in the frenetic exercises of stage hypnotism.

I have had the opportunity to study people undergoing hypnosis, and it soon became obvious to me that they were being put into a trance-like state where the mind partially leaves the body, leaving the brain 'in limbo' and unable to function in the normal way. But that is not all. At this stage, the mind of the hypnotist or the control and the mind of the subject have now become one, in a state similar to the telepathic connection. Unable to function in the physical, the subject takes orders from the mind of the control and, as hypnotists usually have powerful personalities, their subjects are enslaved until such a time as the hypnotist decides to let go. Although this may be similar to a trance state, it is in fact not a trance as we know it, because that is a peaceful experience, and when the mind needs to return to the physical in trance it does so because it has free will. Under hypnosis the subject is a prisoner of the control's mind until he or she is set free.

Most hypnotists have no idea of the complex structure of Mind Energy, which is why some people react badly when they are eventually released from the hypnotic state. I have come to the conclusion, after studying hypnotism for many years, that it is a dangerous practice unless the control has been given the complete medical history of their subject and is adept in tuning into the vibrational rate of that person. This would at least give them an insight into the mentality of the person they are dealing with.

Everyone has a different vibrational rate, and this can be felt by a healer. As soon as someone enters my healing room I can feel their vibrations and can tell within seconds what mental state they are experiencing. Within a moment of laying my hands on them the vibrations change, and I can feel the calming effect of the healing. I can also see their Mind Energy taking on a healthy shape around their head, like a halo. If the patient enters a trance state, the mind will partially leave their body; if it leaves altogether I know that they are in a deep sleep state, where the mind links up with an entirely different dimension. In fact, while in this state, many of my patients have met up with loved ones who have died and who they had thought were gone for ever. The fact that they had free will meant that their mind could decide where it needed to be and for how long, and there was never any question of my patients suffering any ill effects. The outcome was always positive. Much later, they have told me that the memory of the experience was still as positive for them as when it first happened.

The important thing to remember is that these people were not under any control and their minds were free. This is not the case with hypnosis, and that is why it is something that should never be taken lightly. The hypnotic state – where the mind has not completely left the body and there is still an energy connection to the brain – can so easily turn into a 'mind-blowing' situation unless the proceedings are carefully monitored.

It is also extremely dangerous if the subject has an Out-of-Body Experience while under hypnosis. Unless the control is a talented medium, they will not be aware that this has happened and will continue with their suggestions. When someone is having an OBE, it is necessary for them to be in a quiet environment, for example in a meditative state which will enable the mind to return to the physical in a quiet and peaceful way, as it does when awakening from a deep sleep. A bright light at this stage would be extremely harmful to the person's psyche. Experienced mediums are the only people who can detect when this is happening, for there is no machine that can capture the 'out-of-this-world' energy of the mind, not even Kirlian photography.

If the scientific establishment had listened to the talented mediums of the past, they would not have wasted the last hundred years investigating something that involves an energy they cannot see, touch or – without spirituality – investigate. I believe scientists will still be floundering in fifty years' time. There have been – indeed still are – men of science who *are* aware and who, in some cases, are healers themselves. Unfortunately they are in the minority. The majority have closed minds where mediums and healers are concerned, even though we could give them the answers that they spend a lifetime seeking. They believe that if something cannot be proven scientifically, then it is of no value. This is wrong, because the mind is a God-given energy which feeds our inspirational needs, our physical body, and protects us until the day we die when, as an infinite energy, it helps us to leave this dimension and start life anew. As I have said before, their studies are incomplete without the 'knowing' factor.

The scientific establishment is also puzzled about how a hypnotised subject can overcome pain. Again, this is because the mind has partially detached itself from the brain, and the brain is therefore unable to send the impulses that would transmit pain. If the subject is told, under hypnosis, that scalding water is cold, they will believe it.

After many years of ridiculing meditation, doctors are now recommending it to their patients. They know that this practice heals the mind and is an excellent tool for pain relief. They are gradually accepting what mediums and healers have been teaching for many years. But they still don't know how it works. In fact, in a meditative state, the patient is achieving a state of self-hypnosis.

Many years ago, long before I became a medium and healer, I was having dinner with friends when the subject of hypnosis was introduced and the mother of the host kept us spellbound with stories about a particular stage hypnotist. Before hypnotising an eager participant, the hypnotist would ask if they had a telephone in their home, and if there was anyone at home at that time. When he received a positive answer to these questions, he would then hypnotise the subject and ask them to visit their home, to walk through the rooms and give the audience a detailed description of the people in the house, what they were wearing, and what they were doing. He then released the participant from the hypnotic state, and asked if they would mind a member of the audience phoning their home, telling the occupant what had been happening at the theatre and asking for their co-operation. The evidence reported by those at home was the same as that given by the subject. One might think that any accuracy would come simply from a familiarity with the habits of the occupants of the house which would be recalled when under hypnosis. Not so! It soon became obvious that whilst the cat was away the mouse would play and secret habits were disclosed. Although some of the deeds exposed were extremely funny, the lady who witnessed these events assured us that the hypnotist showed great respect to everyone concerned and that no one was in any way humiliated. She also told us this gentleman was an excellent healer, and only used the theatrical performances to support himself financially.

When I began my study of Mind Energy I remembered this story, and it became obvious to me that this particular hypnotist understood the infinite mind and how it can detach itself from the physical, which had led him to the practice of remote viewing. By attaching his mind to that of his subject, he enabled them to mind travel, thus answering his questions at the same time. He did not subject anyone to humiliating experiences and treated them with great respect, because he knew as a healer that he was spiritually committed, which someone must be if they are to control another person's mind.

In a previous book, I have described how I was taken over by a spirit doctor and, through trance, learnt how to give hypnosis. This was not induced by any longings of my own to become a hypnotist – indeed, I was not even remotely interested in the subject. But through my spirit doctor's teaching sessions, I was able to give hypnosis when a patient did not respond to healing. The results were excellent. However, as a result of my own studies, I decided for my own peace of mind not to continue with deep hypnosis, but to just give hypnotherapy, where the subject can be controlled by suggestibility but can still see, hear, and if necessary come out of that state themselves. I also asked my patients to tell me what suggestions they would like me to make whilst they were in that dream-like state. The patients themselves felt more relaxed because they were taking part in their own healing process. I found this method to be extremely successful.

Suggestibility is something that the medical profession and scientific establishment is aware of, and they achieve excellent results when using this method under hypnosis. But there is no need to hypnotise someone to obtain good results with suggestibility – all it needs is a compassionate bonding between the practitioner and the patient.

Hypnotism is a subject that worries me. Of course, everyone has free will, and if they are happy with the practitioner, then so be it. But I still don't think we know enough about mind-altering states to be happy with the situation as it stands at this time.

There is another, darker side to hypnosis, which is the danger posed by the state of the mind of the practitioner, medical or otherwise. There are many sick people around who have the ability to hypnotise. As children we are told that the 'doctor knows best', so that no matter who we are consulting we do not argue, even when our common sense tells us that the treatment offered is wrong, and some terrible mistakes are now being brought to the public's attention. Before having hypnosis, it is necessary to find out what kind of person you are dealing with because his or her mind will temporarily be locked into your own, and in *every* case, a little bit of their Mind Energy will always remain with you.

20

SLEEP

WHY DO WE NEED SLEEP? The mind, brain and physical body have tremendous stamina whilst working in conjunction with each other, but at the end of a twelve-hour day we begin to slow down. The mind – the powerhouse that enables the brain to pass messages to the physical body – cannot sustain the physical body without re-energising itself in its own energy dimension, so as the mind's vibrations become weaker it slowly begins to leave this dimension, and we become sleepy.

Some people can work longer hours than others and seem to require very little sleep. Unfortunately, this will have an effect on their immune system later in life, and the ageing process from fifty years on will be rapid. They will succumb to diseases that they may otherwise have been immune to, and the need to rest during the day will become more apparent. At some time or another, they will have to make up for the years of lost sleep. The stress factor under these circumstances is great, and although the mind comes and goes during the period of rehabilitation, it will take longer for the physical body to rejuvenate itself.

Physical weakness is an issue for everyone who suffers from prolonged insomnia, which proves that there is something missing from their lives that is fundamental to their well-being. That something is Universal Energy. Without it we die. Lack of it can reduce people to the state of walking zombies.

It is essential for those suffering with insomnia to take a walk in the fresh air at least once a day. If for any reason this is not possible, open a window and breathe deeply for ten minutes. If you can do this three times a day, so much the better – it is the finest aid I know for dealing with this distressing state.

The mind is also our guardian, and it can guide us when we are vulnerable. For example, why is it that sleepwalkers can leave their bed and take long hazardous walks, yet come to no harm? The answer is that with the eyes closed and the brain partially inactive, the mind takes over, guiding the sleepwalker through the many hazards that they may encounter.

Another phenomenon which I have already mentioned is the fact that many adults and children have seen me sitting or standing by their beds, not just in this country but worldwide. When someone abroad has seen me standing near them in daylight, I have subsequently worked out the time difference and discovered that I was asleep when the appearance took place. I do not remember these visits because my mind was travelling in an entirely different dimension, and when the mind returns from such travels the pictures become confused when it re-enters the physical body. But I do have the most remarkable dreams, and I know that I travel extensively through them and that I am being protected whilst in this out-of-body state.

I must have experienced strong feelings of *déjà vu* a hundred times or more, and I know it is because I have visited these places whilst I have been sleeping. Some instances have been quite extraordinary – for example, when visiting some homes for the first time, I have been able to give my hosts a list of the contents of their cupboards, attics and garages, places that one would not ordinarily see when visiting someone's house.

Children are especially convincing when they describe places they have seen in dreams. Most are certainly not due to imagination as the descriptions are too vivid, and many of their recollections have been the same kind as my own – not of this world.

There is an old-fashioned saying that if you cannot find the answer to a particular problem then you should go to bed and sleep on it, and you will have the answer in the morning. People did not know *why* the answer would be there, but it invariably was. Through my own mediumistic abilities I know that the mind taps into the Universal Mind whilst it is out of the body and, when it re-enters the physical, the brain downloads the messages and we are made aware of them when we wake. This has worked for me throughout my life. Upon waking, the answer has been so obvious that I wondered why it had seemed so difficult to solve the previous day.

Something that you can do for yourself before you go to sleep is to mentally hand over your problem to whoever is at hand when your mind leaves your body. It is quite simple. When you have closed your eyes, think of the problem you want solved, and say, 'I am handing this over to you. Please help me.' You can then forget it and sleep soundly. If the answer is not there when you wake, rest assured that something will be worked out for you. It does not necessarily mean that you will always be pleased with the result, but it will always – eventually – be for your own good. This is why I impress on others the need to give their problems to whoever may be listening, because if you have faith, there will always be someone there for you.

Many people have seen disasters happening whilst in a sleep state and have thought that they have experienced a nightmare until details of that same disaster have been made public. It may be a day or two later, sometimes weeks or months. I receive clairvoyance all the time through my dreams.

Another aspect of the mind leaving the body whilst one is asleep is the numerous meetings one has with 'dead' family and friends. We meet them all the time in this state, so the contact with loved ones is always there. Unfortunately, when the mind returns the memory of these meetings will not usually remain, because of the difference in the structure of the energies of the brain and mind. But there are times when this is somehow overcome and the memory is maintained. When this happens, the pictures are so vivid and the conversation so clear that there is no doubt at all that the meeting has taken place. It is an experience that one never forgets. I have seen such joy on people's faces when they describe meetings with loved ones they had thought they would never see again. It is possible that these meetings had been planned by the spirit world for some time, but they have to wait until they get the right combination of energies before they can make it happen. Such powers can be as difficult for them to control as they are for us, and like us they have to call in the experts. Life in other dimensions is not that different from this one. The universe is changing all the time and, wherever you are in that sea of energy, you have to 'go with the flow'.

Finally, for any of these phenomena to work for you, you must make sure that your sleeping habits are disciplined. You will look younger, feel younger – and be a whole lot healthier!

21

HORROR, VIOLENCE, AND THE PARANORMAL

I HAVE NEVER BEEN ABLE to watch a horror movie or read a horror book without feeling mentally and physically sick. I have nothing against the people who make the films or write the books. Indeed, I know from my experiences that the majority of people enjoy being frightened. My own feelings of revulsion came as a complete surprise to me, but I cannot ignore the overwhelming and claustrophobic feeling of darkness when I am faced with horror or violence unexpectedly on television or in films.

In my career as a medium I have met many people who, having booked a sitting with me, were quite upset when all appeared to be quite normal – no kaftan gowns, no long beads or earrings, no weird hairstyles (unless I was having a bad hair day!) They obviously needed to be convinced that the paranormal was a frightening experience and, without this massive shot of adrenaline, it simply was not the *real thing*, no matter how convincing the evidence.

Sometimes the sitters brought their own weirdness along to stimulate their adrenaline. For them it was as good as taking a drug. They were high. To an outsider it would have looked as though our positions had been reversed.

Over the years, through workshops, lectures, books and tapes, I have tried to bring a bit of sanity into the equation. It is perfectly natural to be intuitive, which is the first step to being psychic. Very few people laugh when the subject of intuition is introduced in a conversation, but go a little bit further and mention psychics, and the atmosphere changes to one of unease. Mention mediums, and the conversation will more than often end abruptly. Those who argue that mediums are just people who have regular hallucinations are not doing themselves any favours, because it shows that they know nothing about the subject at all. Even worse, it is obvious that they have completely closed minds.

But they are not alone. The makers of horror films often classify their output as 'paranormal'. Television series which are classed as being about the paranormal are, in fact, pure horror. It seems that not only do my clients get the two mixed up, but so do most of the population, many of whom should know better from the evidence of healing. I suspect that using the term 'paranormal' is a deliberate act on the part of the film-makers to attract viewers who would be put off by a 'horror' film. But the label is wrong and misleading. It is also mind-damaging – how can parents prevent their children observing these horrors when the producers of such programmes deliberately mislead the viewers?

It makes me wonder, do people really believe that mediums and healers are involved with horror as shown under the paranormal banner? Our kind of work has already suffered because of misinformation. Our job is to heal the sick and to bring joy to those who have lost loved ones. A talented medium or healer would never introduce the subject of evil into a conversation because they know that the mind can be set on the idea and attract like to like. The energies that surround our practices are peaceful and extremely beautiful – no darkness, only light. If this is not so, then change your healer! The people who make their fortunes out of misleading the public at our expense should be brought to task.

In many ways, these programmes are worse than books and films by gifted horror writers. They at least have the sensitivity to weave their stories into something that is palatable, and because they are talented they do not dish up horror for horror's sake, but rather to make a moral point. They can be subtle and they do not mislead the public, who have a choice over what they are buying. The same choice is not available with television programmes beamed straight into our homes.

Because I have seen the terrible effect that pure undiluted horror can have on the minds of young children – indeed, I have been involved with healing them by erasing the memories they have retained from viewing these programmes and videos – I cannot emphasise too strongly the damage that is being inflicted on them. There are teenage thugs around today who were allowed to watch violent horror films when they were young, and in the process their minds were brutalised. Yet the making of this type of film continues because the programme-makers and stars are making a fortune. They should take some of the blame for the kind of society they have encouraged, but I fear they will not do so because they live comfortable lives, their pockets lined with the gold that has been made from mind-altering films, the effects of which are surfacing with increased violence perpetrated by disturbed minds.

The paranormal has nothing whatever to do with horror. I hope that more parents will complain when they realise that they are being duped and their children harmed by misinformation. Young and old alike are at risk from the disturbed minds of people who have been fed on a diet of horror from birth. If it is not curtailed now the future could prove to be a disaster.

Violence

For years I have spoken out about the violence that is shown on television, video, and in the cinema. Television especially has taught young children that violence is part and parcel of normal life. Well, it was not part of *my* family's life, and I am sure that the same goes for a large percentage of the population. But for decades ordinary decent parents have struggled to protect their children from the violence that they have been able to see by simply turning on the television. Because of this mindless education, children who were introduced to violence at an early age are now committing unbelievably inhumane acts on anyone who gets in their way. One can see from their incredulous or arrogant expressions when they are given a term of imprisonment that they cannot understand why they have been sentenced when their idols, the stars, are given awards for their violent performances. The fact is, these children and teenagers are no longer able to tell fact from fiction. They have been so brutalised and damaged that they have lost touch with reality.

Some programmes now cannot be shown until after nine o'clock. But this is too little, too late, especially for those whose minds have attracted dark forces for so long. Some programmes are going out before the watershed simply by giving violence and horror the heading of paranormal. But once again, the paranormal is about love and light. If mediums and healers did attract darkness in any way, their gifts would disappear, and they would certainly reap a just reward from Universal Law which would render them incapable of practising ever again.

Some films made about the paranormal and mediums during the past few years have been excellent, and they have not only brought laughter to our lives but have also shown the need that everyone has – that of being loved. Films like *Ghost* prove that at least some film-makers are trying to reverse the damage.

However, the dark forces resident in other film-makers continue to give us films of such abominable violence and degradation of the human spirit that one wonders what the people are like who fund these films. How can they live with themselves, knowing all too well that by introducing young minds to these terrible films, future lives are going to be ruined, and innocent victims maimed and murdered. The makers of hard pornography should also take the blame for the terrible damage that has been done to young children. In hundreds of cases, the violence has ended in murder.

The circumstances surrounding acts of violence in the family should be monitored by parents. This is the only way that the first signs of a psychological imbalance can be seen and stopped before it goes any further. Seek help from a counsellor, or from the RSPCA if an animal is being harmed. But do *something*, don't just stand by and pretend it is not happening.

Where the mind is concerned, I can only repeat that one attracts 'like to like'. Universal Law will always ensure that what is given out will return. I believe that this knowledge should be part of every child's education and should be taught in all of our homes and schools.

Throughout the world, terrible atrocities are being carried out in the name of religion. If everyone were to live their lives according to Universal Law, there would be no wars, no atrocities. These dreadful actions would be replaced by love and understanding of our fellow human beings and their right to believe in whatever makes them happy (providing it doesn't hurt anyone else). People would also know that whatever one gives out will join like-minded acts and thoughts, and eventually return to the giver. This is a discipline that needs to be practised by everyone. Many spiritual people have asked me why awful things have happened to them, as indeed they have to me. I give them this quotation, by Daniel Defoe:

> Wherever God erects a house of prayer,
> The Devil always builds a Chapel there;
> And 'twill be found, upon examination,
> The latter has the largest congregation.

141

22

THE UFO PHENOMENON

THOSE OF YOU WHO STILL doubt the existence of UFOs should examine the evidence in the hundreds of books that have been published around the world. You should read the incredible case histories of people who until their encounter had never had any particular thoughts about UFOs one way or another and who are amazed when they listen to the details of their abduction given under hypnosis. They are relieved, too, as it explains lost hours that they had never been able to account for. Many of the scars on their bodies are reminiscent of keyhole surgery. For some the memory of the removal of a foetus, for example, has left emotional scars. Thousands of ordinary citizens have had counselling to help them overcome an experience that has changed their lives for ever. Others describe the love, understanding and a Universal spirituality they experienced when meeting an alien.

UFO formations have been seen and reported by pilots with thousands of hours' flying experience, men of intelligence and integrity. Those with courage stuck to their guns whilst being investigated, while others retracted their stories. No one can blame them. The closed minds of the investigating officers ensured that nothing of value would see the light of day anyway. Valuable information has been destroyed or buried in archives that cannot, at the present time, be accessed. Planes have disappeared after the pilots reported that strange aircraft were tailing them. No trace of those planes or the crews has ever been found.

UFOs have been around for a long time. Even the Bible mentions 'chariots of fire in the sky'. I believe that some of the aliens have been among us for thousands of years, and the reasons for these visits are as varied as the type of alien one encounters – good, bad and indifferent. During the Second World War, a formation of UFOs was picked up on a radar screen in London. Believing them to be enemy aircraft, planes were sent up to investigate. They found nothing, yet the images were still being projected onto the screen. It is obvious to anyone who has studied this phenomenon for a long time that it cannot be dismissed as pure fantasy.

I have seen four UFOs. The most memorable sighting was one that appeared on a still moonlit night over our villa in Spain. (I describe this story in Chapter 5.) I saw two more UFOs whilst walking in a local park. The first one came toward me at lightning speed, losing height as it did so. I put up my hands as if to protect myself and shouted at my companion to be careful. It was only after the event that she told me that she had seen nothing, but admitted experiencing a force that pinned her to the ground. It was extremely unnerving. The second time, I was walking my dog with a friend, and I could clearly see a UFO hovering over the park some distance away from where we were standing. My friend confirmed the sighting.

My fourth sighting occurred years later, when I was sitting with friends in a crop circle. It was a beautiful summer's day, and as I sat down in the middle of the circle I had a feeling of absolute peace and harmony. I placed my tape recorder by my side, and my friends did the same. We were hoping to record the powerful energy that we could feel surging through our bodies. Although many people had given their views about how these circles were made, I was completely neutral. I did not know, and didn't really care – I just loved the beauty of them. The shock came when I closed my eyes and was given a telepathic picture of a spacecraft hovering above us. I opened my eyes, quite expecting to see it still hovering, but there was nothing. Then in my mind I had a vision of lights, similar to wartime searchlights, which were directed at us. Later, when our tapes were played back, mine was the only one to have picked up anything abnormal. It sounded like the hammering of a road drill. I called it the woodpecker.

I knew that Michael Bentine had been picking up a similar sound on his radio, and he had given me an explanation of airwaves that were being blocked by foreign countries. But when I played the sound I had received back to him, he told me that it was unique and that he had never heard anything like it before. (You will find the complete story of this encounter in my book *Mind Waves*.)

I believe that everyone has the right to be informed about what is happening with UFOs. I know life is easier if we can just deal with our everyday problems and have fun in our spare time. Unfortunately, the evidence about visitations from UFOs is over-whelming. No one lives in isolation, and it could happen to you. The people who have described such experiences – especially in the United States, where sightings have become an everyday event because of the vast empty spaces where the UFOs can manoeuvre freely – are not crazy. They are ordinary people.

My own belief is that several species of humanoids have, through mind power, managed to penetrate the different energy structures of the multi-universes. They are certainly dedicated to finding out as much as possible about our planet. Not only do they extract everything possible from Earth, but they also experiment on humans.

Something that occurs both in spirit manifestations and UFO encounters is loss of time. Sometimes it is no more than half an hour but two hours seems to be the norm. Thousands of Americans and some Europeans believe that in this zone of lost time they have had many different types of surgery performed on them. The number of people who have described these experiences is vast. They cannot *all* be hallucinating.

In America, mutilation of cattle is also a large-scale operation, carried out apparently without a shred of emotion. These acts are followed by public outbursts of anger. But who are we to complain when cruelty to animals here on earth has reached phenomenal levels?

These aliens are obviously trying to find out how we survive on this polluted planet. Indeed, many of the telepathic conversations they have had with their captives have shown that they are extremely concerned about the eventual destruction of Earth. Perhaps this is because the destruction of our planet may affect their own Universe, wherever that may be.

People have often seen a ball of light with a tube extending from it, sucking water from a lake, and have wondered why. The extraterrestrials are doing nothing that we ourselves would not do if we were ever able to visit other planets. Our bringing back moon samples is an example – if life *had* been found, samples of that life inevitably would also have been taken. If, at some time in the future, we have a spacecraft that discovers life on another planet, I am quite sure we will carry out experiments, possibly with little or no consideration for the inhabitants.

I believe we should lose our fear of the different humanoids that are visiting us. Being fearful won't stop them coming, and how else are we to learn from them? The few scientists who *have* accepted the challenge have in the past been made outcasts by their universities. Being courageous, however, they carried on with their studies and learnt a spirituality that they had never known before.

The relevance of a chapter on extraterrestrials in this book is because all communication with them has been telepathic – a mind-to-mind communication. I believe that for the aliens, the mind is the supreme power. That is why they can change the shape of their machines, and why they can appear in different guises.

If, as has been suggested, bodies of aliens had been found at Roswell in America, I doubt that any examination would have revealed a body as we know it. Their telepathic ability suggests that their mind power would bypass anything physical.

I also believe that the aliens would not waste their time on people who were unable to receive telepathic communications. Their obvious choice would be those who are already psychic in the intuitive sense, even though the people themselves might be oblivious to this gift.

There have been thousands of sightings of UFOs at places where people know these craft regularly appear, and the aliens rarely disappoint. Their aerial displays are mind-blowing – changing shape, glowing like meteors and disappearing from sight in a split second.

It is all about exchanging information. They are trying to understand us, and trying to help us to understand them. If we do not listen, I believe there will be a much bigger shock for us in the future.

If the world had listened to mediums and healers in the past, it would not now be shocked by the knowledge that there are extraterrestrial beings walking the Earth. Communicating with 'out-of-this-world' beings is second nature to us. Through my books I have been trying to educate the world to the fact that the mind cannot die, that we do reincarnate, that there are others who inhabit the Universe and other universes, and that we are completely insignificant in the scheme of things. It has been obvious to me for decades that the multi-universes and their inhabitants are far in advance of anything we can imagine. I also know that telepathy will be the only language of the future if we are to understand not only each other but also our future visitors. I am also convinced that in time we will be besieged by so many extraterrestrial visitors that our mentality towards these beings will have to change, and fast.

It is encouraging to know that scientists themselves are now calling for a probe into UFO activities.

People from all walks of life and every nationality correspond with me. They are always encouraging me to keep searching for the truth, whatever it might be. They agree with everything I have to say in my books and letters, but they do not blindly believe. Most have had experiences of their own after listening to my tapes, experiences where they have entered a world of peace and serenity that has enabled them to make contact with loved ones they thought they would never see or speak to again. Those who do not get this far find that the tapes give them a glimpse of what might be and have given them a sense of peace. Some have introduced my books into universities around the world, hoping to open up minds that are rusty with age and conformity. The believers invariably outnumber the non-believers in a short space of time.

The scientists who have put their careers on the line by investigating UFOs are experiencing the same hostility that others before them have experienced when investigating the claims made by mediums. The direct voice medium, Leslie Flint, collected hundreds of tapes over the years with the voices of scientists and church leaders lamenting the fact that when they were alive they had '*got it all wrong*'. Their voices were all confirmed as genuine by family and friends. Leslie Flint is no longer with us, but his tapes are – they are a priceless legacy.

It is absolutely necessary for the scientists who are embarking on the very special study of UFOs to bring a spirituality to their investigations. Those who do not embrace spiritual ethics will lose their way, for they are not the kind of people who will understand the essence of our visitors.

I have found that many people confuse spirituality with religion. I know hundreds of people who are religious, but who are not in any way spiritual. Ours minds are of essence, of spirit, and it is what we make of this essence that decides the spiritual or non-spiritual personality. For instance, spiritual people stand by their high principles, even though this stance can cause them dreadful problems. Truth is extremely important to them, and when faced with those who lie repeatedly they experience great distress. Although it may sound strange, spirituality is combined with an enormous sense of fun, because when you are happy with yourself, you can accept the jibes and laughter of others with good humour. Spiritual people know who they are, they know what they ought to be doing, and they are unhappy when they feel they have let themselves down. They know that they will never be perfect, but they endeavour to cause as little hurt as possible in their everyday lives. Spiritual people do not preach but live by example – they leave others to find their own kind of peace.

I have known many pupils who have had their ideas shot down by science teachers. Maybe their ideas were far-fetched, illogical and surprising, but all they got for their searching for knowledge was a sharp reminder that they were out of order. There can be no spirituality where there is not also an open mind. One cannot find the answers in science unless it is linked with spiritual truths. It seems that many teachers fail to give their pupils encouragement, and fail to realise the pupils' basic needs. Perhaps the 'feel-good factor' has gone out of fashion. But if a teacher makes that extra effort and helps a pupil to feel good, then the pupil will put that little bit of extra time to please the teacher. It might be that same pupil who, leaving everyone else behind, finds the meaning of life itself.

You might at this point wonder what spirituality has to do with UFOs. Everything. It can prevent us from destroying them. If a group of advanced people has found a way to alter the atomic structure of energy so that they can slip in and out of dimensions at will, we should treat them with respect and learn from them.

23

MICHAEL BENTINE

THE PERSON WHO BROUGHT light into my life every time I spoke to him was Michael Bentine. Every time I saw him, his bear hugs were full of love and we were always there for each other. When he died, I lost my best friend, and I miss him dreadfully.

I know that he is now with his parents and with his eldest son and two daughters. His son died in an air crash, and his daughters both died of cancer. He loved them so much, as he did his remaining family – his wife, younger son and daughter. They too have lost the light of their lives.

Michael knew that his son was in danger the day before he died. He had been looking down at the floor in his living room and had seen the crash scene etched out on the carpet. He conveyed this psychic message to his son, telling him not to go flying the following day. But all young people dismiss their parents' fears. They feel young and healthy, and do not believe that anything bad can happen to them. It was some time before the plane was found, and we can only imagine the great sorrow that enveloped the family during that time. I did not know Michael then.

I did, however, meet his daughters and was able to give them healing. Unfortunately, it was all a little too late for the healing to have a lasting effect. Once again, the heart of this warm, caring man was broken.

Like all of us, Michael had to pick himself up and go on living.
He worked himself to death on his tours, even though he was
asthmatic. He was always giving, always caring, and always understanding.

But then, when he was in the last stages of his final illness, I
was able to give him something special.

Michael and his wife Clementina had invited me to their home
to meet their American friends. It was a relaxed, pleasant afternoon, but I could see that Michael was not at all well. So I offered
to give him healing, which he loved. This did not affect the
conversations around us at all. The banter and laughter continued
throughout the healing. In fact, I have always found that laughter
accelerates the healing process.

Suddenly, out of the blue, his eldest son appeared in spirit. I
asked everyone in the room to be quiet so that I could hear what
he had to say. 'Tell my mother to warn her brother that he could
be in great danger,' he said. Then he showed me a picture of a
leopard leaping from a tree. As I tried to describe the images being
presented to me, everyone laughed, but Michael told me to keep
listening. His son told me that Clementina's brother was not the
man he once was, that age had taken its toll. He gave me a list
of all the medical problems that his uncle was suffering from, as
though to emphasise the fact that he should protect himself more
than he was doing at the present time. It was quite obvious that
he was not going to leave until he had convinced us all of the
urgency of the situation.

When he finally left, I asked Clementina where her brother
lived. She told me that he lived in Africa, and that hunting had
always been his way of life. Like the rest of us, she knew nothing
about a leopard, or about his current state of health, as he was
not the kind of man who would bother anyone with his problems.
She promised me that she would ring her brother that evening.

Michael asked me quietly whether his son had said anything
about his own health, about whether he was going to recover.

We had always been truthful to each other so I had to tell him that there had been no mention of his illness. Instead, I talked about the evidence we had just been given, and reminded him that if it proved to be true, he could not have received a greater gift. It was quite obvious to me that the message, if true, would convince Michael of life after death, when he most needed that proof. I had seen it all before. From the beginning of the message I had picked up that his son was trying to tell him, in a caring way, that he was there, waiting for him. I believe Michael knew this too.

The next day, I received a call from Clementina telling me that she had spoken with her brother. He had confirmed that, for the first time in twenty-five years, a leopard had been seen in the vicinity of his home. He also confirmed the medical report we had been given, and he was well aware that his physical reactions were not what they used to be. He asked her to thank me, and said that he would take precautions.

As Clementina was always cynical about psychic matters, I pulled her leg and told her that if she did not believe now, she never would. Not one person in that room had any previous knowledge of the information I had received. In fact, we were all dumbfounded, especially as I had been given such an explicit picture of a leaping leopard. Where had that come from?

This story has a sequel. Three months after Michael's death, Clementina called me and said that her brother had contacted her that morning. He had told her that, although he had put bars on the windows of the lodge where he kept his hunting dogs, the leopard had pulled one of the dogs through the bars and killed it. So the warning had been very real indeed.

I wonder, once again, how the sceptics will treat this story. I am sure that Michael is laughing his head off, saying, 'Explain that!' because he was a tremendous support to everyone involved in mediumship and healing. He was a great psychic himself. His father, who was a scientist, was also a psychic investigator, and

Michael had been involved in psychic activities during his adolescence. The stories he told of this time were fascinating and exciting. But Michael the comedian came to the fore when he described the more bizarre people that used to visit.

Because of his early initiation, he hated frauds. When we were talking on the phone one day, he said, 'I wonder if the frauds of this world ever think of the terrible harm that they do to those who are genuine.' I replied that if they did, they would still continue to defraud everyone in their path. There was a moment's silence, and then he said, 'Well, Betty, you and I can't join them, so we'd better try harder at being good.' A typical Michael remark. And I understood. Michael had been defrauded so many times in his life, and so much of his work had been stolen by people who took advantage of him, but like the rest of us he always picked himself up and started again. His sensitivity was such that these incidents hurt him badly though. He could not understand the meanness of some of the people in this world.

Since his death, Michael has contacted me twice. He appeared at my bedside immediately after he died, and again one morning when he asked me to contact his wife and give her a very important, private message that no outsider could have known. I called her and passed on the message, and I think she was suitably shaken. He also talked to her about their family and gave her some good advice, which she subsequently acted upon to her advantage. When I had put the phone down, he gave me some clairvoyance about my future success, for which I was truly thankful.

Michael was, and is, the most wonderful friend that anyone could have had. I miss his physical presence, but I am in touch with his wonderful mind which in my opinion was never fully appreciated by the media. I am also still in touch with his unbelievable sense of humour. His loyalty to his family and friends knew no bounds, but he is still there in spirit, looking after us all.

If I did not believe totally in the existence of an infinite mind,

I would be even more devastated by the loss of this very special friend. It is because of this belief that I continue to write my books, make the tapes, and try to convey to everyone the sheer delight that I feel when I am touched by the mind of such a personality.

I am sure that Michael is still doing his bit to 'make things happen', and I don't think we have heard the last of him.

24

THE MAGIC OF ANIMALS

THOUGH I MAKE A POINT of answering the many letters I receive, I rarely have time to call anyone. But when I received a letter from a man called Eddie Rowan, who lived in Ireland, its contents were such that I decided to speak to him over the phone. He was delighted with the call, and we talked for some time about his problems.

He told me that my book *My Life as a Medium* had completely changed his life – he would like to give something back to others and would like to heal. I told him that he would never know whether he could heal or not until he tried.

He finished by telling me that he was going to get a dog. A few days later he called me. This is his story.

Eddie's story

As you know, we got a little six-month-old Border Collie from a rescue centre on Sunday January 4th 1998. On the Monday night he developed a choking cough, and we arranged an appointment with the vet for Wednesday evening. After arriving at the vet we were shocked when he informed us that Toby had either kennel cough or distemper. He said that both diseases had similar symptoms, except that although antibiotics should clear up both in three to four weeks, the distemper could return, attacking the central nervous system, and could result in the dog's death. On top of this, Toby had also developed a clouding over his left eye which had left him temporarily blind, and both eyes were 'sticking up'. This made him shake violently in order to try and bring them back down so that he could see.

The vet then offered to have Toby put down to save us costs, but I refused. I explained that as well as the medication, I would give him healing and, hopefully, get assistance from a great healer. He looked at me as if to say 'This guy's lost the plot.' On leaving the vet my partner and I felt devastated, but we believed that if anyone could save Toby it would be Betty. So we went home and I called her. I felt terrible when Betty answered the phone because she had lost her voice and could barely speak, but she said she would give Toby immediate healing and that I should give him healing myself.

Toby's room is our converted garage, which has a carpet, two settees and two chairs. After I had spoken to Betty, I did as she asked and went to the garage and gave Toby hands-on healing for thirty minutes. When I went back into the living room there had been no change. Toby was still lying on the settee totally lethargic, and feeling extremely sorry for himself.

As I was sitting in the living room I heard a noise outside and went to look around, but there was no one there. I went back into the living room and sat down. Suddenly, Toby started barking like mad (I must add that until that morning he had never barked at all), and I went into his room to find him jumping from settee to chair and back again, totally crazy. There were cushions, papers and everything else that was moveable scattered across the whole room. The lethargic, sick dog was suddenly totally energetic, hyperactive and acting very strangely indeed. I eventually calmed him down, but he was certainly spooked by something. The room was a total mess, but amid all the chaos I noticed something green sitting neatly on the settee, so when Toby was reasonably sane again I went over and picked it up.

What I had in my hands was a green cloth, folded neatly in four, perfectly pressed and amazingly untouched by the dog's rampage. What was it? Neither my partner nor I had ever seen such an item before. We looked closely, and saw the letters RVH CSSD stamped upon it. We realised that we were looking at a green surgical cover used in hospitals, and that it must have come from the Royal Victoria Hospital in Belfast. So we rang to ask what or where CSSD was, and were told that it was the Central Sterile Surgical Department and that the object we were describing was used only in operating theatres! So where had it come from, and why was this previously very sick dog suddenly full of life?

We both believe that after Betty sent Toby absent healing, one of her spirit surgeons must have visited him and left the materialised theatre gown as proof. I know that with Betty anything is possible – there is no other logical explanation as to how the gown could have got there. From that time Toby has never looked back. One week later, we took Toby to the vet as arranged. This time it was the vet's wife who saw him. When she read the symptoms on the previous week's card she could not believe it was the same dog. She looked at the diagnosis of distemper or kennel cough and said that her husband must have been mistaken, as it takes at least three or four weeks for these symptoms to show any improvement. I told her about Betty and about the incident in Toby's room and, thankfully, she said that she was open-minded but that her husband was a cut-and-dried sceptic. She examined Toby and found that his chest, lungs and throat were all totally clear and healthy, and that while his temperature was still a little above normal – which she put down to his over-excitement at being at the surgery – it had reduced dramatically from the previous week's 104.9°.

What about his eyes, I hear you ask? Well, how does 'bright and moving freely' grab you? The blue cloud has cleared away from his left eye, and he can now see. The vet simply cannot believe Toby's recovery.

I know that spirit surgeons who have been working through me for the last quarter of a century are incredible, and I have no doubt at all that the green gown was their calling card, as similar things have happened a hundred times or more. But I also know that the love and healing Eddie gave was also instrumental in Toby's miraculous cure.

Time and again I have said that those who look over us do not jump in to help every time there is a crisis, but wait for us to take the first step in helping ourselves. Maybe you will have to circumnavigate a dozen or more obstacles, but if you try, you will be given the help needed to overcome the most difficult obstacle of all – self-doubt.

Gill's story

I first purchased Nommie from the riding school I attended in 1988. They had bought her from a horse dealer, when just broken as a five-year-old. Her previous history was not known, but she was listed as a Welsh Cob. Throughout the summer of this year her riding ability was limited. However, we spent many happy hours together and I was able to advance her training until she became adept at dressage, which is unusual for a horse of this calibre.

However, three years later, whilst riding her in the indoor school, Nommie became very distressed. I dismounted immediately as she had difficulty breathing. I took her into the stable yard and, because of the severity of the attack, called the vet. When he arrived he gave Nommie an injection and put her on medication. She was not ridden for some time. From time to time she seemed to recover, but then the symptoms would return with a vengeance. Eventually I asked the vet to give her a thorough examination. The diagnosis was not hopeful, as she appeared to have a lung complaint which is similar to the human form of emphysema. I spoke to the vet for some time, and it was obvious that Nommie's riding days were over. I was most distressed.

At this stage I read about Betty Shine and her ability to heal animals. I wrote asking for absent healing for Nommie, and Betty replied with the comment 'healing has commenced'.

From that time on Nommie improved daily. I continued to extend her rides until she was cantering around, and I kept in regular touch with Betty.

All horses at the stable have a yearly medical. When Nommie was examined by the vet he was most surprised to find her breathing normally and her condition so improved. He found her fit and well enough to continue normal working.

Now, ten years later, I have given up riding, although I am still Nommie's owner. She is part of the team at the riding school and she delights in giving rides to the disabled – and they love her. In the summer she loves to canter on the beach.

I still have regular contact with Betty and do not hesitate to ask for help when needed. I know it will always be there for humans and animals alike.

Mieke's story

I received the following story from Mieke Frankenberg (see Chapter 15), which her daughter Annie Gould had kindly typed up for her:

When I met Betty Shine at the RAF Club, I asked about something that had happened years ago to that day. My husband, who had lung cancer, had gone into hospital to have a bronchoscopy, which was going to be carried out the following day. After settling him in at the hospital, my daughters and I went on to a charity evening at the Royal College of Obstetricians. Annie rang him from the College at 11 o'clock, and he told her that the anaesthetist had given him the go-ahead and that he would be first on the operation list the next morning. He said he was going to sleep. Forty minutes later I arrived home and my little dog started barking very loudly, scratching the carpet, trembling, running through the rooms and up and down the stairs. I picked her up, but she would not stay. Then the phone rang and I was told that my husband had died a few minutes before. When I finished telling Betty this story she said that she was not at all surprised, that such things happened all the time. Animals are naturally telepathic, and can sense when a spirit is present – when my husband had died, his mind, being free, had simply come home.

In a note accompanying this excerpt, Annie wrote, 'Whilst typing Sally's story for your book, I reached the part where Mummy talked about her dog's reaction when Daddy died, and my own dog – who had been lying quietly by my feet – suddenly went crazy and started haring around and around like a mad thing!'

When I had finished reading Annie's letter, I rang her and explained that just by thinking of her father she had attracted his spirit to herself and her home, and that the dog, like her mother's, could see him. Animals do not like strange things happening around them. It is natural for them to communicate telepathically, but when they are confronted by a mind that is not connected to a physical body, they go haywire.

My own cat has always been able to see spirits, and by now she has seen hundreds. But she has never been afraid of them and stalks them as though they are some kind of prey. She will also sit on the top of my chair when there is a spirit entity around and stare at it so intently that she does not move a muscle. Even when it has disappeared she will still sit glued to the chair, just staring. Perhaps she can still see it when I cannot; perhaps she has the ability to see forms of energy that I cannot. Who knows? There are times when I know that she has gone into a trance, and that her Mind Energy is not there; when this happens she looks like a statue.

When I receive a letter from an owner asking for healing for an animal I connect up mind-to-mind with the animal, initiate a telepathic connection, then carry out distant healing. That way I can pick up so much more information than the owner can give me. Sometimes the problem is caused by stress, especially if there are several children in the house – animals do like their peace – or perhaps it is caused by an aggressive atmosphere in the home. Telepathically, animals are extremely communicative, so when they give me an insight into their lives I am given the whole picture, and then I can heal them. If I can pass on the information received without causing distress to the owner, I do so. If not, I will try and get around it somehow. I encourage the owners to watch their children, if there are any, as well as other adults in the family, to see if anyone is aggravating or hurting the animal. Children are noisy and boisterous, and though adults accept that, animals do not understand our ways and have to be protected and nurtured. Humanising them can be marvellous for us as they adapt to our lifestyles, but they are still animals, so please show them respect and give them some time to themselves. At least give them time to release their minds, and leave them in peace when they are sleeping so that they can roam in the world of free spirits. Like us, only there can they have the freedom they deserve.

25

CLAIRVOYANCE AND INTUITION

I T IS WELL KNOWN THAT I dislike giving clairvoyance. Perhaps my reason for this is not fully understood, so in this chapter I thought I would endeavour to rectify this.

I am a deeply spiritual and truthful person, so when I was asked to give clairvoyant sittings at the beginning of my career I was happy to do so. I knew I only had to relax and send my mind on a journey to get results. The pictures I received were quite incredible and I was able to give my clients an extremely detailed account of their past and future lives, including the many pitfalls they would have to endure and the ultimate conclusion of the particular phase they were living through at that time. It soon became clear to me that the people who had great unhappiness in the past would continue to suffer in the future, because of the rigid mind blueprint they had fashioned for themselves from childhood. Everything was so clear to me that I was able to pinpoint the exact nature of their past actions and give them invaluable advice about how they could change their thinking to enjoy a happier future. It came as a shock to me to find that about eight out of ten of my clients did not want to change in any way, did not want to accept that they could have been wrong at any time in their lives, and certainly did not want to be told that there was anything in their future that could cause them distress. They wanted the rainbow's end, nothing less. In fact, it was obvious that they had already decided what they wanted to hear even before their appointment.

This was a real dilemma for me. Although my friends and dedicated clients told me that my clairvoyance was spot on, and practically all the people eventually confirmed that everything had happened as predicted and now wanted to come back for more, I began to dislike the sessions. I was a healer, first and foremost. The last thing I wanted to do was to make people unhappy.

I could quite understand how some psychics gained their bad reputation. They simply told people what they wanted to hear. That way their clients would leave with a happy smile and would feel that the visit had been worthwhile, when actually it had probably been an expensive and useless exercise which would only be shown in its true light when the golden future turned out to be pure dross.

Although I never relished clairvoyant sessions, I did learn from them, because it became increasingly obvious that I was not receiving clairvoyance by telepathic means but by the ability to scan past and present in different dimensions. I was told repeatedly by my clients that the clairvoyance they had received had little to do with their lives and that my predictions could never come true. At the same time, I had absolute faith in my visions and knew beyond a shadow of doubt that they would become a reality in the future. My belief in the infinite mind grew stronger every day. Because the messages and visions seemed to have nothing to do with the majority of my clients *at that time* and obviously had nothing to do with telepathy, the messages had to be something that could travel in a different time frame. The connection with Universal time and our own time, a way of looking back and forward, something that fused it all together, had to be the infinite mind. It was free energy that kept us in touch with not only our past and future in this life, but also with our past lives.

People change all the time, and I have found that this goes in seven-year cycles. If we do not change with these cycles, and accept that our attitudes, habits and dreams have to change with them, then our lives are going to be pretty chaotic. Nothing stands still. Nature is always changing. New leaves replace old, seemingly dead shrubs burst into life, shoots from bulbs deep in the earth reach for the light. A new beginning. We should take a leaf out of nature's book.

With the information received in clairvoyant sessions I was able to help the most negative clients by impressing upon them the need for change, showing them how to build a mind blueprint that would give them a more exciting and positive future.

I also found with women that it was their driving need to please that caused most of their illnesses, unhappiness and general frustration. With healing and counselling I was able to show them that no one in this world can please everyone, that we all have to have an escape route where we can simply *please ourselves*. When they adopted this attitude, the change was incredible. They were happier, their families and friends were happy for them, and most important of all they were fulfilled – and they did it themselves. All I gave them was a magic box of tricks – thought forms that they could shape, project and use to remould themselves and teach those around them to do the same.

The most frustrating part of clairvoyance is the fact that it is extremely difficult to give an exact timing for future events. Time, as we measure it, is man-made, but the information we receive is from another time frame, another dimension. Man has drawn up time maps of our Universe, but with clairvoyance, mediumship and healing, we are not in tune with our own dimension but with entirely different levels and energies. These can only be scanned with the mind, because that is the only tool we have that enables us to explore other dimensions, other Universes. I have found that I can link actions, past and present, into our time frame, but only when I am given the information in my role as a practising medium.

I believe that many sceptics would be amazed by the number of people who long to have psychic power. Just counting those *I* have met runs into thousands. But if you think of the words 'psychic power', they automatically give the impression of a formula that could help one to scale the heights without too much effort – and they unfortunately attract those whose basic need is to control others. However, unless you are prepared to commit yourself to years of training and spiritual awareness and to abide by Universal Law, you will not acquire this talent.

There is an easier path – using the lower level of your natural psychic ability, namely intuition. We are all intuitive, but most people seem to have lost the art of listening to their inner voice. They ignore that very special 'gut' feeling and prefer to listen and act on advice from others, often with dire results. If you want to take better control of your life, do not ignore your gut feelings, because they will usually be right.

What *is* gut feeling? It's as though someone has taken your insides and twisted them. Don't mistake it for pain, for it is not painful. It is an uncomfortable 'knowing', and you ignore this feeling at your peril.

As a medium, when I have taken note of my gut feelings I have been okay, and when I have ignored them the outcome has been disastrous. But, like the rest of humanity, I am only human, and emotions can play havoc with logic.

Another incredible aid that your intuition will give you is the 'immediate response' which you might experience whilst in conversation with someone. You will receive a thought so strong that it will feel as if you have heard the spoken word. Some people actually do hear the words. If this happens to you, you'll know that your intuition is working well. For example, your immediate response might be that someone is lying. Take note, hold on to that thought, remember it. Don't tell anyone else about it, for this will immediately weaken the impact of your own unique intuitive gifts. Simply retain the information and keep it for future reference. It may keep you out of trouble in some way.

These immediate responses can come at any time. You may be driving along in your car and about to turn a corner when a powerful thought enters your head that there is a car parked in a dangerous position just around the corner. It all happens very quickly, but it would obviously be advisable to slow down as you turn that corner. My own life has been saved several times by reacting rapidly and positively to my intuition.

If this technique helps you become a more successful human being by listening to your inner voice, keep it to yourself until you have become comfortable with your ability. Like everyone else who shapes their lives in this way, you will probably have to take a lot of flak from others. In their ignorance and jealousy, they will try to wear you down. Just keep them guessing as you add more zest to your life!

When, through practice, you have absolute faith in your abilities, you will find yourself developing unique feelings of your own. You may feel the hairs rise on the back of your neck – a negative response. You may feel an upsurge of joy – a positive response. If you have an uncomfortable feeling and somehow feel 'itchy', don't make any decisions at this time but leave them until you've had time to think things through clearly. These are examples that others have experienced, but they may give you some idea of what to expect. However, it is quite easy to work out what type of reaction you are experiencing. A joyous, happy feeling is extremely positive. An uncomfortable feeling in any form, is negative, while a 'fidgety' feeling requires further investigation. Keep notes about your reactions so that you can refer back to them later.

I hope these suggestions will free you from dependency on others. However, by using your intuition you will also have to take responsibility for your own life, which means that you will think before you act and not the other way round.

I have been asked many times how intuition works. It is quite simple. By listening to your feelings, and taking note of them, you automatically release your mind, at which point it expands and touches the Universal Mind, and information is received. With practice and relaxation, your mind might continue to expand, and you may eventually become psychic.

26

CLONING THE MIND

I DO NOT KNOW WHY such a fuss was made about the cloning of Dolly the sheep. Human beings having been making a success of a different type of cloning since the beginning of time – not physically, but with the mind. The nature of my work has brought me into contact with hundreds of clones. Unfortunately, these people were not aware that constant companionship had encouraged their Mind Energies to link up more often than was healthy for them.

Twins, for instance, are not just linked genetically but become inseparable because their minds have been as one both in the womb and out of it. As children they are encouraged to wear not only the same clothes but also the same colour. If they are identical twins, people even in the same family may become confused and mistake one for the other. This encourages the cloning still further as the tiny children cling to each other, too young to sort the problem out for themselves. The confusion can sometimes last into their teens and beyond. In my practice I have met twins who have been unable to make even minor decisions without referring to their other half. They also feel that when they are apart they are living in a dreamworld. This is because one mind does not want to let go of the other, and when this happens it results in an imbalance. Fortunately, in most cases it does not take long to adjust naturally. It is not a dangerous situation, and there are thousands of twins who are happy with the way they feel because they don't know what it is like to feel totally independent. Eventually the time will come when one of the twins dies, and this can be a dreadfully upsetting experience. Not only does the survivor have to deal with losing their soul mate, but they themselves have to adjust and become a whole person for the first time in their lives. I have often been told, by a twin who has been left behind, that it feels as though their mind is incomplete, that a part had died. And so it has. I have explained that they were correct in their assumption, as their twin had taken a little bit of their Mind Energy with them.

On the positive side however, the ability to link up mind to mind is a lot easier for twins than it is for most people. I have explained to them that their minds, linked for so long in this world, would always be seeking the other and that they would never really be apart. For example, when we are born we take a bit of the Universal Mind so that we will always be linked with Universal energies, without which we could not survive on this planet. Their twin, therefore, will always have a link with the other no matter where they are in the Universe.

This has been proved many times by survival evidence given to the remaining twin, because the evidence has been so detailed that it could only have been given by someone in close contact with their soul mate. It also makes it easier to teach the remaining twin how to communicate telepathically; after all, that is how I receive survival evidence from the mind-to-mind contact with the deceased. In fact, I have taught this method of communication to many twins who were finding it impossible to function on their own.

I have also impressed upon them that just as one has begun a new life in another dimension, so the other must also start anew and become a unique personality in their own right. With help, most of them have achieved this and, in so doing, have tasted freedom for the first time. Many remarked that they would have liked this to have happened whilst their twin was still alive. This can happen naturally, if one twin has a stronger personality than the other, but it can also occur if they have knowledge of Mind Energy and act accordingly. With this knowledge there is always a choice.

Cloning of the mind is also obvious where there is a dominant partner in a relationship, or a particular member of a family; in too many cases, the weaker partner is given no choice in the matter.

Perhaps the reader would automatically assume that the controlling influence would be a man, but this is not necessarily the case. Because my sight goes beyond the physical, I can detect the energy of the personality, which is mind, and can give an immediate diagnosis. I have seen men who, although large in stature and with an arrogant, know-all personality, have been terrified of their wives and who have displayed a weakness of mind that is almost unbelievable. Most of these men had married young, when their personality was undeveloped, and had simply found it easier to fall in with their partner's wishes rather than try to oppose them. As mature adults they are unhappy, because they have had to forego their own principles in order to pacify their partners. The worst cases I have seen are where a husband defends his wife to the hilt in front of friends and family but completely ignores the fact that their actions and words have caused terrible pain to others. Eventually, their family and friends will disappear, and who can blame them? No one needs such dreadful aggravation. This can be a tragedy for all concerned, because with a little thought and concern for others it could have been avoided.

On the whole it is women who are more likely to sacrifice their own personality and allow their partner to capture their minds. Eager to please, women have a history of becoming martyrs to the cause. Most adolescent girls are hungry for love, and to receive this gift they believe they have to be subservient to their mate. I have seen young girls who parents have instilled certain sets of principles, hoping that if their daughter lives by these principles then she will find happiness. Most parents spend their whole lives worrying about their offspring. Along comes a young man, who has no principles, who is offensive and dismissive, but who captures the young girl's heart, and overnight her parents are faced with a nightmare. For the gift of love, the girl has allowed someone to connect with her mind, take hold and refuse to let go. Personalities cannot make contact with the brain, which is, after all, physical tissue, but they can easily invade the energy of the other mind with their own – and within a short space of time the partner has been 'cloned'.

In my healing practice I have counselled thousands of adolescents and their families who have found themselves in these situations. I have seen the devastation caused by the undesirable effects of mind-to-mind contact. Because of my ability to affect energy I have sometimes been able to bring about a happy conclusion for everyone concerned. But there is no greater devil than that of obsession, and no greater enemy of the open mind than that of the obsessed. They cannot bear to be parted from the dominant companion because they have allowed them to affect their mind and soul. Obsession, whether it is with a good partner or bad, is not conducive to good health, even though it may seem wonderful at the time. It is better to become close friends and cosy soul mates at the first opportunity.

I think the worst case of cloning is that of the intelligent man or woman who allows themselves to be put down all the time and who agree with their partners – in public and in private – to avoid constant arguments and humiliation. They are being abused. I have, over many years, seen the tragic outcome of these so-called partnerships.

If you wish to avoid becoming a clone, then think. Do not continually agree with your partner if you think he or she is wrong, and have the courage to say so. It is easier sometimes to agree on small things to keep the peace, but *keep* it to the small things in life and think things through for yourself if you feel unhappy with a major decision. You may find that you make a bad decision, but how else can you learn if you do not try? Intelligent people are not always right, and will admit to their failings and learn by them. Beware the person who always assumes that they are right. Steer well clear, because these people can be dangerous.

I have always found it very sad when one partner falls out with a friend and expects the other to do so as well. As unique individuals we cannot always like the same people, and you should be allowed to keep a friendship alive. I have known many people who make friends, allow them to become bosom pals, then – without a word of explanation – do not speak to them again. It is an abominable way to treat people. Yet they do not stop, they go on and on, making friends and dropping them. In such cases perhaps the other half of the partnership should have the courage to explain to the injured parties – who deserve an explanation – what is going on.

I have also observed 'cloned' friends and partners following every kind of so-called new therapy that others in the pack have found. They rush around from therapist to healer, to mediums, hypnotists, counsellors, acupuncturists, herbalists and medical specialists of all kinds until another new name or idea is introduced. It does not really matter what the new trend is called, they will try it.

Dependency on anything is weakening. Try to work things out for yourself. Feel unique and you will be unique. But most of all, think for yourself. If you find yourself being drawn into a world that is abhorrent to your own sense of right, then keep your distance. It is difficult sometimes to do this, especially if you have fallen madly in love and passion overshadows your reasonable and logical thought. But there are times, even in these situations, when you will have some thinking time to yourself, and it is in these quiet moments that you should bring yourself to take a good look at what is happening. Know, deep inside, what you are prepared to lose before you continue on what could be a mind-wrecking experience. The passion *will* eventually subside, because the physical body simply cannot continue to give so much all the time. Hopefully the end result will be a calmer love, where true affection replaces lust. Whatever happens, remember that you are unique to yourself and that, because of your principles, there are certain lines you will not cross. In this way you can keep a scrap of sanity whilst in the throes of a passionate affair.

More important, do not ignore close friends at these times. If you do, you may lose them forever – believe me, you will need them again later.

Mind cloning does happen. Know that it happens, and protect yourself. We all have the right to freedom of mind, word and deed, and we all have the right to choose our own friends, no matter what others may think. Never accept as gospel what others may say about friends and family, but check it out yourself, and reach your own conclusions. Free your mind and you will be a happier, healthier human being.

27

NON-VERBAL COMMUNICATION

I HAVE ALWAYS BELIEVED that the world would be a better place if intuition was combined with verbal communication on a day-to-day basis. Unless you are particularly psychic, it is extremely difficult to *know* when someone is lying to you, but if everyone practised listening to their intuition, we would instinctively know who we could trust and who we should avoid.

From time to time you will meet people who try to blind you with science. If they happen to be one of your family (or even worse your boss), you may have to listen to their theories. But if you are completely at ease with your intuition you will not be taken in. This will give you the confidence to stay cool and to remain polite. Then when you are alone you can make an assessment from what you received intuitively with a little bit of logic. This way you have the best of both worlds.

Ignorance can also play havoc with our intellect. If you suddenly find yourself having to answer awkward questions on a subject which you know little or nothing about, listen to your inner voice and you will soon find yourself responding with a reasonably intelligent answer.

Listening to the audible silence around you is evidence that you are relaxed. In this state your Mind Energy expands and begins to touch the dimension of Universal Mind. In other words, you are reaching out and making contact with like minds. Once you have touched the source, you can extract the knowledge. When you become adept, this will happen so quickly that you will begin to wonder where the answer came from. Each day of your life will become an adventure of the mind. This is only the first step – the more powerful you become, the more expansive your mind will become, until you begin to develop clairvoyance or 'clear vision'.

Intuition, clairvoyance and the 'knowing' instinct will give you freedom of thought, word and action. But you will also have to take on the responsibility of self. You will no longer be able to blame others for your mistakes, because you should have known better. If you go into a situation, either financial or emotional, then you must realise that you alone bear the burden of responsibility. If things go wrong, take the blame and begin anew. A fresh start is always exciting, after all!

No matter who you are or what you do, you will make mistakes, but intuition and common sense will teach you more about the world than any teacher ever could. With the help of your 'gut feeling' (see Chapter 26, 'Cloning the Mind'), it is possible to distance yourself from situations that can be extremely damaging and dangerous – ignore such intuition at your peril.

The people who reach the top in their professions have an intuitive knowledge of 'self'. When they are with others, they speak the words and walk the walk, but behind closed doors they dream their seemingly impossible dreams. They know that 'gut feeling' and 'knowing' can make those dreams come true. They have proved to themselves that the first thought that comes from that 'knowing' will be the right one, and that if they try to argue with it and reach a different conclusion it will be wrong. That is why they are sitting in the Chairman's office and you are not.

Having said that, if they are the kind of person who abuses these gifts, then they will lose them. Ego is not compatible with the spiritual realm, and the ego will lose every time. There have been so many famous people who have lost out because of their egos – we all know people like this.

It would be interesting to make a note of those who have fallen by the wayside, and those – who may be perceived to be just as egotistical as their counterparts – who are still surviving. Having studied this particular aspect of life for many years, I know that in these cases you cannot take it as read that they have hidden qualities. Ultimately the egotists will lose one way or another. Materialism cannot buy friendships, and their world will become a very lonely and loveless place.

It is important to note once again that spirituality is what you make of your mind, which is essence or energy. It is not a religion, for they are all man-made. Spirituality is quite different, and the basis of it is knowledge. Seeking knowledge, so that you know the difference between right and wrong, is the most important task you have whilst you are inhabiting this planet.

I know that I repeat this more times that you would like to read it, but remember Universal Law, that whatever one gives out will return to the source. If you are someone who is dreaming the dreams but they are not happening, everything could change overnight, because it is only with practice that intuition thrives and expands. Eventually, you will feel the power, and hopefully by the time you reach your goal, you will have learnt much from those who have fallen on barren ground.

Because we cannot escape our emotions, they become the trickiest thing to deal with. I have been asked many times how this equates with people falling madly in love with the wrong person, especially if one half of the partnership is otherwise particularly intuitive. The answer is that the intuitive partner knew they were making a mistake but decided to go ahead because of their deep need for love and physical contact. They had the gut feeling but ignored it – and so they had to live with the consequences.

This brings me to the subject of freedom of choice. It is always there, because we have freedom of thought, but if something goes radically wrong with your choice you cannot blame it on intuition, for when you are accomplished in this art it will never fail you. You will have to blame *yourself* for making the wrong choice.

It is worth the effort to study the effect of intuitive gut feeling, starting with relatively unimportant choices. First of all, think of something not connected with your choice, so that you take your mind away from the subject matter. Then think of your choice and stay with that thought. Write it down and date it. Carry on in this way for about a month, and then study the consequences of your choice. If on a scale of one to ten (for a good result) you can award yourself a mark of seven, then you're doing well. Continue in this way throughout the following months, and you will see how your intuition becomes second nature.

Telepathy

I have had conversations with foreigners where they have been struggling with English, yet the content of the communication has been perfectly clear. Words were unnecessary. Because these people were eager to speak with me, they unwittingly transmitted their unspoken thoughts in conjunction with their words. When I made them aware of what was happening, most of them were astonished that they could reach me in this way, and felt slightly embarrassed. After all, telepathic people are considered a bit odd, aren't they?

Well, that is what the world has been told, mainly by scientists, who should know better. For if some scientists of the past had not fallen asleep in their laboratories and communicated tele-pathically with like minds, we would still be groping in the dark. Thomas Alva Edison was the first to admit that it was only after waking from a deep sleep that he realised he had been given the answer he needed in connection with his lightbulb theories. Born in Ohio in 1847, he was expelled from school for being retarded.

That is the first clue to his psychic abilities, because most psychics are not natural academics and usually listen to the audible silence for their answers, using their intuitive and telepathic abilities with like minds in other dimensions. It was because of his natural psychic abilities that he became the most prolific inventor the world has ever known.

Albert Einstein also admitted that he had only found the answers to some of his theories (one of which was the theory of relativity) after he had fallen asleep in his laboratory. He was a mathematical physicist and did much to enlighten man's understanding of the Universe. In 1921 he won the Nobel Prize for his work.

Nostradamus (or Michel de Notredame) was a doctor of medicine. Interested in astrology, he set himself up as a prophet. His predictions were so accurate that he earned himself a great reputation. To this day people still read his books and take note of the clairvoyance he has given for the future.

Michael Faraday, English physicist and chemist, has materialised to psychics many times. One famous professor, a friend, was helped in his own work by Michael Faraday and claims to have seen him materialise many times whilst he was working in his laboratory. Michael Faraday discovered electromagnetic induction and invented the dynamo, and Faraday's Laws of Electrolysis demonstrated the effect of magnetism on polarised light. It is no wonder he needed to materialise – what more proof does one need?

The fact is that many scientists are also natural mediums. Earlier in the book I said that mediumship is akin to physics and that scientists should think carefully before they dismiss this. After all, mediums often look as though they have fallen asleep when they go into trance whilst communicating with spirit beings – I believe Edison and Einstein were natural mediums.

There is no doubt that the ability to communicate without words is so powerful that it has to become part of everyday life if this planet and its inhabitants are to survive. As with everything else in life, ignorance will stand in the way of every door that leads to enlightenment. But we have the knowledge to fashion our own keys to open the many doors of the mind. It is never too late to learn.

28

RECLAIMING YOUR LIFE

AT SOME POINT IN YOUR LIFE, something will happen
that will turn your world around and make you think. Only
then will you realise that by continually ignoring the thought
process, you have walked into a potentially damaging situation,
not only with your eyes wide open but, far worse, with a closed
mind. Very few people escape this process, and it can happen
when we least expect it. At this point, many of you will be telling
yourselves that this could never happen to you. But please read
on.

If you become ill, what is the first thing you do? Do you take
an alternative remedy that you have in the home? Do you visit
your doctor and hope that he can shed some light on your problem? Perhaps you decide to read a medical dictionary and make
your own diagnosis, or seek advice from a friend? Depending on
the kind of ailment that you have, one or all of these remedies
could be the correct action. but there is something missing from
the equation, something that is so obvious that you have probably
never given it a thought. Your lifestyle.

I am only addressing minor complaints in this chapter, because
if you can stop this process at the outset, many of the major
medical problems simply will not happen. However, I believe you
can take a number of steps towards better physical and mental

health. Study the following exercises carefully. They will help you change your life.

First step

The first step in reclaiming your life is to arm yourself with an exercise book and pen. Don't use a pencil, you may be tempted to rub something out. When you have acquired these items, begin the analytical process by underlining the heading, which will be MATERIALISM.

List everything you have bought in the past twelve months, apart from the usual day-to-day goods that we all have to buy, on the left-hand side of the page. If you wish to take your time and be specific, this may take several days. When you have finished, return to the top of the page and, on the right-hand side, write against each item how many hours you or your partner have had to work to acquire it.

Second step

When you have finished both lists, start a new page and write down the heading LOST TIME, LOST LIFE and underline it. Then put down everything you would have liked to have done, either with your partner or with friends and family, if you had not been working so hard for your acquisitions.

At this point I will remind you why I asked you not to use a pencil. This is because pencil can be erased, and the words you may wish to erase could, if studied carefully, be the turning point in your life. Look at them and ask yourself how and why they have appeared on the page. Why do you want to erase them? Do they disturb you? If so, then you must look at why they are creating a disturbance. After all, the words are only there because you put them there. They could be the something that you have been deliberately ignoring because you could not face up to the consequences, or they could be meaningless at present but a warning sign for the future. They may even be positive words that foretell a happy, healthy future. Whatever they are, ignore them at your peril, because they are a form of clairvoyance, of 'clear sight'.

Third step

Now turn to a new page, write down the heading AILMENTS and underline it. Then list all the ailments you have suffered during the past twelve months. Ask your family and friends how they would sum up your general health during those months. It is quite normal for us to try to block out the unpleasant things in our lives, especially illnesses, and others may help give you a clearer picture.

Fourth step

Study all the exercises over a period of a week or more. Do not rush this stage. Take your time. Only when you have made an honest assessment of everything you have written down can you turn to a new page.

Fifth step

On your new page draw several horizontal lines across the paper, leaving at least two inches below each line. It is important to note that what you put underneath these lines will affect your future life. Write STRESS on the top line – it represents how much stress and ill health you are prepared to suffer for the type of lifestyle you have at the moment. Ask yourself whether you can honestly sustain it, knowing the full facts, because if you cannot, you know that your immune system and your mental health will suffer. Put down YES or NO on the line. If the answer is YES, you will know that you have given a lot of thought to the answer and that you are in control of your life. However, it would still be in your best interest to read on, to find out what your future may hold.

If the answer is NO, then decide which material possessions you could do without so that you can enjoy more stress-free hours with your family and friends. Write them down in the space below the line.

Sixth step

Go down to the second line and decide what INITIATIVE you are going to take so that you will have more control over your life. For example, if you have suffered more colds, coughs and flu than those around you, you will realise that your immune system needs a boost. Go to your local health store and look at the numerous books they have on sale. Choose one and read it. When you have done this, write the title of the book underneath the second line. I guarantee that you will be determined to find out as much as you can about preventative medicine and that you will end up adding more titles to your paper.

You may of course suffer from a number of allergies, in which case the above advice will be the same. Remember, allergies are also a sign of a weakened immune system, and any kind of stress will set them off.

Seventh step

Acquire as much knowledge as possible about MIND ENERGY, for this will be the heading on the third line. Read how, with positive thought, you can prevent the build-up of blockages in the energy system which, above all, protects our minds and physical bodies from rapid deterioration.

Further steps

If you have been able to go through all the steps and make decisions that will change your life for the better, then you are on the road to reclaiming your life.

If you wrote YES on the top line at the beginning of the fifth step, be sure to re-evaluate your life from time to time. It could be that this practice may help prevent unexpected ill health or disasters in the future.

Those of you who want to live a more simple life should carry on with the process, moving further down the page as and when you have achieved the knowledge and self confidence to do so. You could use the following headings to explore yourself.

Emotions

Emotions are difficult to control. But if you want a healthy life you must put the brake on extreme reactions. If you are faced with this problem in others, you must simply keep out of their way. There is no greater enemy to our mental and physical health than the negative forces that are released when the atmosphere is charged in this way.

Expectations

Do not blame others when your expectations of them fail. The only true expectations you can have are those you have for yourself. If they fail, then you can only blame yourself and try to do better next time.

There is no way that you can always succeed, but it is extremely rewarding when you do.

Do not lie down

Throughout your life you will have to take many knocks. When this happens, get up. If you are knocked down again, get up again. Others will weary of the game before you do, and it will show them how much resilience you have when you believe in yourself.

However, if it becomes obvious that someone is out to destroy you, you may have to leave a job, a partnership or a new project. Whatever it is, leave the scene with dignity and put your faith in Universal Law. No matter how long it takes, the perpetrator will eventually receive their punishment from this source – one cannot make deals with Universal Law.

Possessions

Do not be taken in by other people's lifestyles. They may have bigger houses, servants, better paid jobs, expensive cars and so on, but these do not necessarily make for a happy life. If you are a decent, caring individual you will probably have more love in your life, even if you live in a bedsit. Of course there are decent people living in those big houses but, on the whole, one cannot have fame and money without having to give up one's privacy. There is always a price that has to be paid.

Do not let jealousy mar your life. Use your intuition when meeting someone for the first time. If you have a distinctly uneasy feeling, then no matter what they have got, or where they live, you should not have them as a friend. Trust your own judgement.

We are all unique, and we all work best at different levels. Somewhere in this chart you will find your level for a stress-free life. Unfortunately we all have failings, so you should re-evaluate your life every six months or so. In the meantime, the following proverbs and calming thoughts might help you to deal with everyday problems.

Proverbs

A word spoken is past recalling.

All that glitters is not gold.

All things come to those who wait.

Nature abhors a vacuum.

Love begets love.

If at first you don't succeed, try, try, and try again.

Hasten slowly.

More haste less speed.

The unexpected always happens.

There are two sides to every question.

To err is human; to forgive is divine.

Cut your coat according to your cloth.

You must take the fat with the lean.

You never know what you can do until you try.

Zeal without knowledge is fire without light.

Wise men learn by others' mistakes; fools by their own.

Civility costs nothing.

Comparisons are odious.

Barking dogs seldom bite.

As you make your bed, so must you lie on it.

A penny saved is a penny gained.

A man is known by the company he keeps.

A fool and his money are soon parted.

Beggars can't be choosers.

Better a devil you know than a devil you don't know.

Forgive and forget.

It's the pace that kills.

No gains without pains.

In the country of the blind the one-eyed man is king.

It takes two to quarrel.

History repeats itself.

Hypocrisy is the homage that vice pays to virtue.

Ill-gotten gains never prosper.

Manners make the man.

Moderation in all things.

Little strokes fell great oaks.

Lend your money and lose a friend.

Let them laugh that win.

No man is wise at all times.

The wish is father to the thought.

Rats desert a sinking ship.

One swallow does not make a summer.

Prevention is better than cure.

Practise what you preach.

Respect a man, he will do the more.

Remove an old tree, and it will wither to death.

Use pastime, so as not to lose time.

When one door shuts, another opens.

Calming thoughts

Give love wherever it is needed.

Look at the earth during the day, and the sky at night. Then you will always have something beautiful to behold.

With a touch of class you will not only look good, you will feel good.

Be kind to yourself.

Don't beat yourself, or allow others to do so. You are worth more.

There is a message in every book.

Those who think they know it all know very little.

Always leave the doors of your mind open.

Love comes in many guises.

Don't prepare yourself for the worst. Expect the best.

A smile can brighten the darkest room.

Money cannot give you happiness. You have to find that for yourself.

Don't try to win every argument. And you will live longer.

Meditate at least twice a week. It will save your sanity.

Add something to this list every day and analyse it. Eventually you will have a clear picture of what you really want to do with your life.

29

BE TRUE TO YOURSELF

FORTY-FIVE YEARS AGO I became involved in vitamin and mineral therapy. Having cured myself with a vitamin supplement, I studied every book that I could find for more information. There were very few in those days – in fact, Barbara Cartland was the only other person who was writing about this therapy, and it was from one of her first pocket books that I found my own cure.

Over the years I successfully treated my own family and friends, and anyone else who was interested. But the sceptics seemed to be creeping out of the woodwork every time this kind of therapy was mentioned, and the medical profession was positively scathing. My own GP told me that it was absolute rubbish when I told her I had cured myself of a complaint that she had not even been able to diagnose. I read all the books written by the Shute doctors who practised in America. They were a family of heart specialists, and their studies of vitamin E were a revelation. The Shute Foundation for Medical Research has no commercial interest and is supported by public subscriptions and fees of patients.

I also studied cell therapy, after which I recommended vitamin E in various strengths to everyone I met, because it protected the body from the free radicals that caused oxidation of cells. Antioxidants include vitamins and minerals which protect the centre of the cell by neutralising the free radicals. Uncontrolled free radicals form when people are exposed to smoking, alcohol, medicinal drugs, irradiation, the absorption of heavy metals, pollution, sunlight, and more. We are all at risk from pollution of the atmosphere. We cannot escape, and that is why antioxidants are a necessary supplement.

There is a constant war going on in the body, but there is a good chance of healthy survival if one takes antioxidant supplements. It has been said that the use of antioxidants in the future could be the breakthrough that the medical profession has been waiting for. It could have happened sooner if they had listened instead of dismissing such new ideas as rubbish.

I have been recommending vitamin E as a preventative measure against cancer, arthritis and a host of other conditions for over forty years. It amuses me, therefore, when I read medical reports in newspapers and in science magazines that state that a certain doctor or scientist has found that antioxidants, and vitamin E in particular, are beneficial to our health. However, I do not in any way belittle the work that they are doing to advance our knowledge in this field. I still want to know more, and I am sure that people today want to take advantage of the facts – make no mistake, antioxidants are the finest prevention supplements that we can take, and I have always maintained that this is so.

Remember, however, that the pioneers were battling against cynicism from every corner a hundred years ago and deserve much more credit. For instance, one Dr Shute told the story in a book of how heart disease increased over a hundred years ago when bread was refined for the first time. The life-giving substances in natural bread were bran and vitamin E. These were taken out by removing the bran and the wheatgerm, the source of the vitamin E. Vitamin E is the heart vitamin, and bran prevents colonic cancer by internal cleansing.

I also read a book about forty years ago that told of a man in Yugoslavia who was about to have a leg removed because of gangrene. He decided to go home and think about it. Whilst he was sitting watching his bees coming and going in their hive, he thought about the sterility of the comb inside the hive. How *could* it be sterile with all the bees carrying their pollen to and fro? Then he watched as they landed on the sticky mass at the bottom of the hive, the mess that all beekeepers hated to clean out at the end of the season.

He went indoors and found a small bottle into which he poured alcohol, then made his way over to the hive and took a small piece of the sticky mess from the bottom of the hive and put it into the bottle. He left it to soak for two days, and then started to take a few drops a day. Within a week the gangrene started to clear and eventually disappeared. He had saved his leg.

Of course this made headlines. Scientists in Switzerland tested the substance, and found that in some forms it was stronger than streptomycin. That was the birth of Propolis. Now that the medical profession have been advised not to give out so many antibiotics, Propolis will come into its own. You can take it every day as a tonic, and it is a natural antibiotic.

I was interested in a newspaper article which told the story of a group of nuns who gave Propolis to their patients, most of whom were suffering from senile dementia and Alzheimer's disease. They found that there was a definite improvement in their patients' health and memory, and now the results are being evaluated by a medical team.

I could write so many stories about vitamins and minerals, but I would like to end here with Ubiquinone Q10. No one should be without it. It not only provides body fuel but is one of the most powerful antioxidants that we have. It is expensive, but you can always think of something that you can go without. Q10 is a must. Some of the diseases that can be helped by taking it are alcoholic cardiomyopathy, arthritis, auto-immune illnesses, catar-acts, diseases of the liver and heart, emphysema, inflammation, multiple sclerosis, senility, premature ageing, and many more.

Athletes who go in for hard body exercise should certainly take it, because the more you push your body in this way, the more free radicals you will produce.

I have been true to my beliefs for nearly fifty years. I have been maligned for my beliefs. Now I have proved that I was right, and I can stand alongside those people with open minds who did not let the critics deter them, and who gave us all so much that we could work on.

Have faith in yourself, and always have an open mind which will take its strength from the Universal Mind. *The Infinite Mind*. There is no finer source.

30

THE PLANET IN PERIL

IT IS A FACT THAT MORE and more people are suffering from allergies, especially babies and small children. Their parents also suffer as they try to find a cure. I have seen children covered with open abrasions due to eczema or gasping for breath when having an asthmatic attack. There are hundreds of ailments due to allergic reactions, especially to food that has been sprayed with chemicals throughout its life.

Every month hundreds of people are suddenly and dramatically crippled by severe stomach cramps. They are advised by medical consultants and alternative medicine practitioners to avoid wheat, and then they take this advice the problems disappear. But at what cost? Reading the labels on food packages, you will find that most of them contain wheat. It's extremely difficult for those afflicted with a wheat allergy to have a wholesome, interesting and tasteful diet. Our bodies are overloaded with wheat, which could be one of the reasons the allergies develop, but I also think there is a more sinister reason for this dilemma.

Wheat is sprayed with chemicals, from the planting of the seed to the harvesting of the crop. When it rains, these chemicals are washed into the ground and not only neutralise life-giving substances but are taken up into the crop itself. When the crop has been harvested it is stored in silos, where it is repeatedly sprayed to kill beetles and weevils. This practice alone could be avoided, especially since scientists have found that storing grain at a low temperature would kill off the bugs. But most of the silos are old and farmers cannot afford to update them.

In Chapter 10, 'A Whole Bag of Tools', I explained the treatment I give in the 'Mind Medicine Room', which can be extremely effective in allergic reactions. The mind is a useful tool in self-healing, but it is the underlying cause of these allergies which should concern us most, a never-ending list of physical problems – including cancer – from chemicals like organo-phosphates. The problem is that chemical fertilisers have neutral-ised natural selenium in the soil. Studies on cancer victims have shown that they have no selenium in their bodies, and the same results have been found in those suffering with all forms of arthritis.

Forty-five years ago I was petitioning with other like-minds to ban DDT. Sprayed around the globe like water on every little patch of earth in our homes and gardens, it was obvious that everyone in the world would at some point ingest this chemical. After many years it was banned in this country, but not before it was discovered that everyone living in so-called civilised society had DDT in their tissues.

My daughter Janet and her family were in Turkey recently, and as they walked to a local village were shocked when they were surrounded by a fog of chemicals being sprayed around a campsite. The chemical was DDT. The fog spread into a nearby town, and they could smell it for miles. I found it hard to believe that the campers would willingly stay on a site that had been contaminated in this way, and that babies and small children – as well as adults on a supposedly healthy holiday – were deliberately being subjected to this inhumane and dangerous treatment. The whole world is aware of the dangers of this chemical, and yet there are whole continents ignoring these dangers.

Our real enemy is greed. There are people in top professions – scientists, manufacturers, drug companies and politicians to name but a few – who ignore the whole ecological disaster for the sake (as the Americans would say) of big bucks.

Many years ago, after the ban on DDT, dieters in this country were advised to lose not more than one pound per week because of the danger of too much DDT being released from the fat content of the body, where it was stored, and to prevent a poisonous reaction.

I have spent my whole life encouraging people not to use insecticides, to make up natural sprays and to cultivate an organic approach to everything they grow. Yet these insecticides are used constantly, sometimes in the confined atmosphere of a room where they can do most damage to the occupants. I cannot understand why people are quite happy to inhale poisons that could eventually kill them rather than let a few flies land on their windowsills.

How many times have you eaten food sprayed by an overzealous host who is intent on killing every fly that lands on it? Unfortunately for the diners, the food is instantly contaminated by poison, and they could be harmed by eating it. There are so many simple ways to keep insects and flies off food, in the home and garden, such as decorative mesh food covers which can be bought cheaply anywhere.

The hospital tests that are used to detect allergies are excellent and where there is a bad reaction the offending substance can be avoided. But I have known some people who have apparently been allergic to dozens of different things and whose lives have become a living hell. It was not until they came to see me that they recovered, helped by energy alchemy, which can change the biochemistry of the physical body.

For many years I have peeled every piece of fruit I have eaten, but it seems that even this is still not enough. In America it's been found that poisonous sprays have seeped through the skins and the fruit itself has become contaminated. This comes as no surprise to those of us who have fought for so long to prevent the contamination of crops and the soil and to protect the health of future generations. Whatever is being done now to counteract the madness that has turned our world into a chemical cesspit, it is too little, too late. The way out would need every politician to believe in the power of the mind and the alchemistic nature of that energy to produce miracles. Unfortunately, politics are about ego, and the ecological disasters going on around us do not seem to interest politicians. Perhaps they think that taking a stand will make them unpopular?

I have mentioned in previous books the harm that is being done to people who work and live in the vicinity of power lines. Until now, this has been dismissed, but at last it has been proved that the magnetic forces around power lines attract pollution. It seems that the contamination that the power lines attract can be drawn in from an area of three miles or more.

Mediums are able to diagnose ecological problems many years before they eventually come to light. I have been giving information about ecological disasters for years to anyone who would listen, but unfortunately it is the very people who should be listening who won't heed a medium's advice because of their own standing with the establishment. It is their loss – but it is ours too.

I have had many conversations with people in power in different countries. They have admitted that although they are aware of the special information that talented psychics can give, such information would be dismissed because of the source, yet these very same people have sittings, healing and clairvoyance. They have told me that the so-called logic of their opponents would always win over the more free-thinking individual, but if they all had the courage to band together and stand fast against the majority, the world would be a more enlightened place. No one is asking sceptics to *believe*, but they owe it to the people they govern to at least *listen*. It could be that they would learn something not only to their advantage but to the advantage of the whole world.

My thoughts on this subject are perhaps best summed up by a poem which I wrote many years ago:

> I have walked a million miles
> and seen a million things
> that have disturbed my inner being.
>
> The ecology of the Earth disrupted,
> a vicious circle of stupidities
> and man's inhumanity to man.
>
> All natural instincts crushed
> by en masse education,
> the tenderness of youth
> destroyed by facts and figures.
>
> Where pernicious influences
> of the outside world had
> not yet reached, only there,
> did I find peace.
>
> And when the Earth has finally
> turned to dust, only then,
> will we realise, we have killed
> the only source from which we feed.

31

TOUCH

PEOPLE TOUCH AND HOLD each other too little in this life. Sometimes it is only when someone is close to death that they receive a kiss or a hug. I don't think one can say that this comes too late, because such demonstrations of affection are better late than never. But it would be nice if you could give more love to those close to you whilst they can still fully appreciate it.

Children and old people like to be touched. The warmth and natural healing qualities that we all possess should be passed on so that those on the receiving end will feel happier, healthier and loved.

From the thousands of letters I receive each week from around the world I know of the terrible feelings of isolation, of loneliness and of being unloved that are experienced when someone lives alone. And this is so much worse when one is old.

For some reason, touching seems to be a cause of embarrassment for a lot of people in this country. Perhaps it is the climate that makes us appear outwardly cold, or perhaps it is the strange admiration many people have for the 'stiff upper lip'. Certainly the Mediterranean races – Spaniards, Italians and Greeks – suffer from no such inhibitions, and you do know exactly where you stand with them. So let us take a leaf out of their book and accept the fact that touching is therapeutic.

There are some people who simply do not like to be touched. How does one get close to them? The answer is to mentally shroud them in blue energy and see that energy being absorbed by their bodies. The transformation in these lonely people can sometimes be extremely dramatic. I have seen men, in particular, react very quickly: where there had been no chance of a smile, they have laughed; where there had been ho hope of being touched by them, they have hugged; and where there had been pain and misery, healing had taken place. 'But I am no healer,' I can hear you saying. Wrong! Everyone can be a channel for healing. All it needs is love and compassion in your touch or thought, because love is the greatest healer of all. If you have love and compassion, then your Mind Energy will expand and – in so doing – pure love will be channelled through you to be passed on. And don't worry about doing too much. When the energy counterpart of your patient has absorbed enough energy, it will close down until the next session. You will know when that happens as you will intuitively withdraw your hands.

If you happen to be a long way from the person you would love to heal, then give them distant healing. My discovery and study of Mind Energy over the past twenty-five years has proved that 'The thought is the deed.' Sometimes the healing arrives before the thought has been completed, but rest assured that your loving thoughts and prayers *do* reach the people you love, and they do make a difference.

You may be surprised to know that by healing others you are also healing yourself. When the healing energy passes through the chakras and meridian lines it will automatically remove blockages from your own system, and allow your major organs to vibrate and to regain their health.

Throughout my career as a healer I have been amazed by the number of young people who write to me asking for healing for a friend or a member of their family.

They have also told me about the healing they are giving, by following the instructions in my books, and about the elation they have felt when they've been successful in alleviating or curing their patient's problems, especially if the patient is a beloved parent.

I am sure that the love received by those around them was deeply appreciated, especially as some of the healers were below the age of eight years old! That, surely, is pure love.

These healers are too young to feel embarrassed, and they use their gut instinct in their desire to heal their loved ones. I hope they will never change, for they are our future.

32

A New Beginning

PEOPLE CRACK WHEN they are in the depths of despair. Yet it is at this precise time, when the 'cracking' releases them from the materialistic ego-ridden prison in which they have lived, that they experience a rebirth, a new beginning.

Unbeknown to them, it has all been stage-managed by their higher mind – the part of the Mind Energy that touches the Universal Mind. In these dimensions, clairvoyance can determine which route the soul needs to take in order to prevent the premature destruction of the whole.

Light can only be seen in all its glory when it shines in the black depths of human consciousness. Once this has been experienced, it will never be forgotten. The road to enlightenment is never as severe as the road to self-destruction.

Some people may wonder what fun they can get out of life if they take the path to enlightenment. The answer is simple: you will begin to smile again. You will learn the art of laughing at yourself and at the stupid actions your super-ego demanded you take. Laughter is the beginning of all healing.

If you can turn self-love into a giving love, this will also ensure that you will have a safe journey. And you would be well advised to avoid the ignorant and the foolish who cross your path, until you are strong enough to resist the urge to preach, for their experiences will differ from your own.

Love

Many people believe that we can only reach enlightenment through suffering. This is not so. As a healer I have experienced a pure love which heals, and the process changes both the healer and the healed forever.

If you have been scarred by life, think only of love and light and the scars will disappear. By using the Infinite Mind in this way, you can become your own Alchemist.

APPENDIX A

PASSAGES FROM THE BIBLE

I think there is a message in these passages for everyone. And every message will be different according to the needs of that person, or the justification of their acts. The passages are from Paul's letter to the Corinthians, chapters 12–14, quoted from the New International Version of the Holy Bible.

Spiritual Gifts

Now about spiritual gifts brothers, I do not want you to be ignorant. You know that when you were pagans, somehow or other you were influenced and led astray to dumb idols. Therefore I tell you that no-one who is speaking by the Spirit of God says, 'Jesus be cursed', and no-one can say 'Jesus is Lord', except by the Holy Spirit.

There are different kinds of gifts, but the same Spirit. There are different kinds of service, but the same Spirit. There are different kinds of working, but the same God works all of them in all men.

Now to each one the manifestation of Spirit is given for the common good. To one there is given through the Spirit the message of wisdom, to another the message of knowledge by means of the same Spirit, to another faith by the same Spirit, to another gifts of healing by that one

Spirit, to another miraculous powers, to another prophecy, to another the ability to speak in different kinds of tongues, and to still another the interpretation of tongues. All these are the work of one and the same Spirit, and he gives them to each one, just as he determines.

Excerpt from One Body, Many Parts

And in the church God has appointed first of all apostles, second prophets, third teachers, then workers of miracles, also those having gifts of healing, those able to help others, those with the gifts of administration, and those speaking in different kinds of tongues. Are all apostles? Are all prophets? Are all teachers? Do all work miracles? Do all have gifts of healing? Do all speak in tongues? Do all interpret? But eagerly desire the greater gifts.

Love

And now I will show you the most excellent way.

If I speak in the tongues of men and of angels, but have not love, I am only a resounding gong or a clanging cymbal. If I have the gift of prophecy and can fathom all mysteries and all knowledge, and if I have a faith that can move mountains, but have not love, I am nothing. If I give all I possess to the poor and surrender my body to the flames, but have not love, I gain nothing.

Love is patient, love is kind. It does not envy, it does not boast, it is not proud. It is not rude, it is not self-seeking, it is not eagerly angered, it keeps no record of wrongs. Love does not delight in evil but rejoices with the truth. It always protects, always trusts, always hopes, always perseveres.

Gifts of Prophecies and Tongues

Follow the way of love and eagerly desire spiritual gifts, especially the gift of prophecy. For anyone who speaks in a tongue does not speak to men but to God. Indeed, no-one understands him; he utters mysteries with his spirit. But everyone who prophesies speaks to men for their strengthening, encouragement and comfort. He who speaks in a tongue edifies himself, but he who prophesies edifies the church. I would like every one of you to speak in tongues, but I would rather have you prophesy. He who prophesies is greater than one who speaks in tongues, unless he interprets, so that the church may be edified.

Now, brothers, if I come to you and speak in tongues, what good will I be to you, unless I bring you some revelation or knowledge or prophecy or word of instruction? Even in the case of lifeless things that make sounds, such as the flute or harp, how will anyone know that tune is being played unless there is a distinction in the notes? Again, if the trumpet does not sound a clear call, who will get ready for battle? So it is with you. Unless you speak intelligible words with your tongue, how will anyone know what you are saying? You will just be speaking into the air. Undoubtedly there are all sorts of languages in the world, yet none of them is without meaning of what someone is saying. I am a foreigner to the speaker, and he is a foreigner to me. So it is with you. Since you are eager to have spiritual gifts, try to excel in gifts that build up the church.

For this reason the man who speaks in a tongue should pray that he may interpret what he says. For if I pray in a tongue, my spirit prays, but my mind is unfruitful. So what shall I do? I will pray with my spirit, but I will also pray with my mind; I will sing with my spirit, but I will also sing with my mind.

APPENDIX B

My Law

The sun may be clouded, yet ever the sun
Will sweep on its course till the Cycle is run.
And when into chaos the system is hurled
Again shall the Builder reshape a new world.

Your path may be clouded, uncertain your goal:
Move on – for your orbit is fixed to your soul.
And though it may lead into darkness of night
The torch of the Builder shall give it new light.

You were. You will be! Know this while you are:
Your spirit has travelled both long and afar.
It came from the Source, to the Source it returns –
The Spark which was lighted eternally burns.

It slept in a jewel. It leapt in a wave.
It roamed in the forest. It rose from the grave.
It took on strange garbs for long aeons of years
And now in the soul of yourself It appears.

MY LAW

From body to body your spirit speeds on
It seeks a new form when the old one has gone
And the form that it finds is the fabric you wrought
On the loom of the Mind from the fibre of Thought.
As dew is drawn upwards, in rain to descend
Your thoughts drift away and in Destiny blend.
You cannot escape them, for petty or great,
Or evil or noble, they fashion your Fate.

Somewhere on some planet, sometime and somehow
Your life will reflect your thoughts of your Now.
My Law is unerring, no blood can atone –
The structure you built you will live in – alone.
From cycle to cycle, through time and through space
Your lives with your longings will ever keep pace
And all that you ask for, and all you desire
Must come at your bidding, as flame out of fire.

Once list' to that Voice and all tumult is done –
Your life is the Life of the Infinite One.
In the hurrying race you are conscious of pause
With love for the purpose, and love for the Cause.

You are your own Devil, you are your own God
You fashioned the paths your footsteps have trod.
And no-one can save you from Error or Sin
Until you have hark'd to the Spirit within.

TIEME RANAPIRI

If you wish to receive distant healing, or book and tape brochure, please write to the address below:

Betty Shine
PO Box 1009
Hassocks
West Sussex
BN6 8XS

For homeopathic advice, send a separate letter addressed to:

Betty Shine
(A.G.)
PO Box 1009
Hassocks
West Sussex
BN6 8XS

Please keep letters short and enclose a stamped and addressed envelope.
Thank you.